GUIDELINES FOR CONTEMPORARY CATHOLICS:
Suffering and Evil

John Heagle

THE THOMAS MORE PRESS
Chicago, Illinois

ISBN 0-88347-212-0

CONTENTS

To Keith,
who carried our questions to God.

Introduction

NAMING OUR DARKNESS

THE questions which surround suffering and evil are as old as human awareness. From time immemorial women and men have asked, "Why?" as they witnessed the suffering of innocent people or reflected on their own pain. Every generation has had its share of families and individuals who have grieved quietly in the face of senseless death or cried out in helpless rage against the night. There have always been bleeding bodies, starving babies, and broken hearts. The river of sorrow is as old as humanity.

All the same, there is something different about the manner in which we confront evil today—something more poignant about our fears and more urgent about our questions. The issues may be fundamentally the same as they have always been, but the stakes are much higher. In our time we face the issue of suffering and the problem of evil not just because it is intellectually challenging, theologically significant, or personally compelling. We must examine the question of suffering and evil because our very survival is at stake.

Only a few months before the 1986 disaster at the Chernobyl power plant, a Soviet scientific journal published an article reassuring Russian citizens and the world about the safety of nuclear energy. The authors stated that there was only one chance in ten thousand that a real crisis could arise and even then the technicians had back-up mechanisms with which to deal with such an event.

As we know all too well, the unexpected took place. The

one event in ten thousand did in fact occur. In a critical chain of events the system broke down, the back-up mechanisms failed, and a major catastrophe took place. The immediate destruction which came in the wake of that tragedy was widespread—probably more widespread than we are aware. But the long-term damage to human and animal life, to the earth and its environment, is only beginning to come to light. It is impossible to calculate at this point the effect which this will have on the health of the Russian population surrounding Chernobyl. Nor can we yet measure the long-term impact on the farm land and the wider environment. There is already evidence, however, that the effects of this disaster will be widespread and enduring. In Norway, where the prevailing winds carried the initial fallout, the levels of radioactivity are so high in many of the sheep and cattle that the meat from these animals is not considered safe for consumption. Radiation has affected the reindeer population of Lapland so seriously that it threatens the genetic future of the species and the entire way of life of the Laplanders, whose culture and survival are linked to the reindeer.

The significance of Chernobyl goes far beyond the apparent failure of Russian technology or the global struggle between the super powers for strategic advantage in the arms race. Chernobyl is a moment of truth for humanity in the 80's, just as Hiroshima and Nagasaki were moments of truth in the 40's. Beyond the devastation which occurred at the time, these tragedies have become a grim reminder that we have entered a far more intense confrontation with the mystery of suffering and evil in our time than ever before in history. They are symbols that the age-old questions have new implications.

In the early days of human civilization people found it convenient to blame their misfortunes on the gods or fate; there was a strong tendency to blame the world or nature. In our own Christian tradition it was often God or "original sin" that took the brunt of responsibility. Today we no longer have the gods or the furies or fate to accuse. Nor would it occur to most of us any longer to blame nature. We are left with God and ourselves—the divine promise and our human fragility. Mostly we are left with the gift of freedom and responsibility which God has given to us to tend the earth and to build the kingdom. In some profoundly mysterious way, we now have history in our hands. The future is, more than ever before, our responsibility.

This is a chastening and sobering realization, and one with which we do not necessarily feel comfortable. Not too long ago we were heady with a Promethean sense of our technological power and the coming of the secular city. We were confident about the possibilities of scientific progress and our capacity to overcome some of the ancient diseases and limitations which have traditionally plagued the human condition. But recent events have changed all that. We are more cautious in our forecasts and less confident about our technological powers. "If the Sixties was an age of naive hope," writes novelist David Leavitt, "then the Eighties is an age of ironic hopelessness."

But Christian faith calls us to hope, not despair; to engagement, not withdrawal; to humility, not arrogance. The issues of human responsibility and the capacity for evil are too important to leave them to fate or to those who seek to rule by dominative power. The church's teaching and our personal call as Christian disciples echo a common invitation to reflection and creative action. This is an age when we must name our darkness and carry our responsibility for the future.

It is in this spirit that I approach the mystery of suffering and evil in this book. Like the other volumes in this series, this study is an attempt to provide a framework for deeper insight into our tradition, as well as an opportunity for personal growth in faith and a shared reflection on the major theological issues of our time. This book will explore the question of suffering and evil within the tradition of the Roman Catholic faith, with its roots in the Hebrew and Christian scriptures, and the historical development of these issues in the lives of believing people. It will approach these questions not only in terms of their biblical, theological, and doctrinal content, but also in terms of their personal meaning and the shared call to action which is ours as Christians in our time.

Chapter 1

HOPING AGAINST HOPE

The Experience of Suffering and Evil

KEITH was the kind of child every parent wants. He was cheerful, bright, initiating, and in love with life. His classmates in the first grade loved him, his teachers were proud of him, and his grandparents tried their best to spoil him. All of us marveled at his youthful insights into God and life. I smiled in amazement when I discovered that he had enthusiastically prepared to celebrate his first Eucharist a full year ahead of time.

One balmy evening in late April, Keith left the house to ride his bicycle. On his way back to help with the supper dishes, in an instant forever locked in his mind's eye, Keith swerved into the path of an oncoming motorcycle and was thrown unconscious onto the pavement.

I found Keith's mother and father in the surgery waiting room when I arrived at the hospital a short time later. For the next three hours we waited helplessly while a team of doctors performed emergency surgery. During those long hours we alternately prayed and wept together. There were periods of stunned silence and some small talk, as if to reassure ourselves that somewhere there was normalcy. I remember thinking that this must be what Paul meant when he spoke of "hoping against hope" (Rm 4:18). Finally the neuro-surgeon appeared in the doorway and spoke quietly to Keith's parents. He told them that ninety percent of Keith's brain was damaged beyond repair and had to be removed. It was unlikely, he said, that Keith

13

would live; and even if he did, he would never have a normal human life.

We stood in the hallway as Keith was wheeled past us on the way to the critical care unit. Up to that point I had been praying that Keith would live and, if possible, recover fully from the accident. Now I no longer knew what to pray for. Part of me, I know, began to hope that God would take him into eternity.

Contrary to medical expectations, Keith did not die. When the respirator and the other life-support systems were removed, he began to breathe on his own. After two months he was moved from the hospital to a health care center for neurologically handicapped children. Keith can still manage a smile, especially when his family brings him home for a holiday afternoon, and he has been able to learn how to chew and swallow his food. On occasion it almost seems like he understands and remembers, but for the most part there is a deep silence in his eyes. A year after the accident, when his classmates were preparing to celebrate their first Eucharist, Keith's parents brought him to the chapel at the health care center. Surrounded by his family and the health care staff, Keith shared the Lord's supper and smiled broadly.

Unless there is a miracle, Keith will spend whatever remains of his life at the health care center. He will not be able to follow the dream that was already forming in his heart before the accident. He will never ride his bicycle again or play outside with his friends. He will never be able to sing the music he loved or read the books he cherished or speak his heart to another human person.[1]

The story of Keith has its parallels in other families and in the lives of people throughout the world. His life is not the first or the only one to be crippled by a senseless accident. There are countless other children in the history of humankind who have died of starvation, pestilence, war, and abandonment; who had no one to care for them, let alone remember them. If it is possible to measure suffering, there may well be more tragic profiles of human anguish than that of Keith. After all, someone might argue, Keith still has the devoted love of his parents and brothers; he is cared for by a competent and professional staff of people; he is in comfortable surroundings and does not experience much physical pain.

But knowing all this does not take away the grief or the sense of loss for those who are thrust into the reality of suffering. The story of Keith is important, not because his is the only or the most dramatic account of suffering, but because he and his parents are people who are actually walking through the reality of pain. In their flesh and daily concerns, they are living the mystery of the cross. Their pain and their sense of loss are real; so are their faith and courage.

Any understanding which we can gain from studying the theological implications of suffering and evil must find its roots in life—in the actual experience of pain. It must involve real people whose grief and anguish reach beyond the limits of philosophic argument, scriptural exegesis, and doctrinal statements. It is too easy for us to intellectualize the meaning of suffering or to turn theology into an academic exercise. This is not to underestimate the serious and reflective task of theology; it is simply to locate the starting point of such reflection in the mysterious complexity of human experience.

When we know someone like Keith and his family and

enter their journey of faith, the issue of suffering can no longer be reduced to the search for rational answers. Some instinct tells us that we have entered the realm of mystery. The questions which have haunted human hearts from the beginning become *our* questions. We feel them in our depths before we pose them with our minds. They rise up in us like a tide of emotion that must find expression: Why is there so much needless suffering in the world? Why do the innocent die without the opportunity to live productive lives? Why do the wicked appear to flourish and find prosperity, while the just live in squalor and oppression? Why do our prayers for our loved ones seem to go unheeded? Where is the God of love and compassion in our time of need?

These questions are as old as human memory. So too, it appears, is the attempt to answer them. If there is a history to the questions, so there is also a history to the answers. Usually the search for an answer to suffering and evil takes place in the context of religious faith. The great religions of the world provide us with varying responses in doctrine and practice to the mystery of evil. Obviously, our concern here is with our own religious heritage, the Judeo-Christian tradition. In addition to the questions which we share with the rest of humanity, there are some that are unique to ourselves.

How did our ancestors in faith, the Hebrews, view the reality of human anguish? How did they understand the meaning of death and disease and the oppression of the innocent? How did the understanding of God's relationship to suffering and sin begin to change, and why? Did Jesus "solve" the problem of evil? In what way is his life and teaching a response to the great questions of human life? Is it possible to believe in a loving and good God and at the same time reconcile ourselves to the reality of evil and suffering in our world? What is the teaching tradition of the Catholic church regarding the problem of evil? What are contemporary theologians and philosophers saying about the issue? What is the framework of faith in which I can shape my personal response to the painful aspects of human life? These are some of the questions that we will explore in this study.

Before we address these questions, however, it is important to "prepare the ground" by making some preliminary reflections. This initial discussion is intended to help clarify some of the language and concepts which will be employed in the following chapters.

The Context of Faith

The focus of this study is the meaning of suffering and evil as it is experienced in the framework of *faith*. We begin with the assumption that there is no satisfactory rational explanation for human suffering or for the reality of evil. In other words, we are not as much interested in an intellectual "solution" as we are concerned about discovering a way of responding to the presence of evil and of living creatively with its consequences. Jesus did not say, "I have explained the world;" but he did say, "I have conquered the world" (Jn 16:33). As believing Christians we are challenged to embrace and to live the meaning of this victory over suffering and evil.

All the same, we are creatures who ask questions and seek for answers to our dilemmas. Even as we try to live the Christian mystery we also want to understand it more profoundly. We may not regularly employ the tools and sophisticated language of the sacred sciences, but every serious Christian instinctively pursues the same goal as theology: *"fides quaerens intellectum"*—faith seeking understanding. Thus we will also explore the classic and contemporary responses which have been developed for the problem of evil. We recognize that we are walking on the holy ground of mystery, but this does not excuse us from the distinctively human task of questioning, doubting, and wrestling with the mystery which envelops us.

The Relationship Between Suffering and Evil

There are some theologians who contend that suffering is related to evil but not necessarily synonymous with it. To suffer is to undergo physical, mental, emotional, or spiritual pain, injury, or loss. Not all evil entails suffering for the person or persons who are directly involved. It is difficult to know, for instance, how much Keith actually suffered at the time of the accident, or how much he is aware of suffering in his present circumstances. But even if there were little or no suffering on his part, the painful reality of evil still confronts his family and friends and all who know him.

The same is true in the widely publicized case of Karen Anne Quinlan, who, before her death in 1985, existed in a comatose state for more than a decade. The medical evidence seems to indicate that she did not suffer during this period of time, and yet her potentialities and dreams went unrealized. In other words, we instinctively recognize that evil is evil whether or not it causes conscious pain for the person who undergoes it.

Can we maintain, therefore, that not all suffering is necessarily evil? This questions becomes especially significant when we know people who have conquered disabilities and overcome physical or psychological handicaps to accomplish great things for humanity. In some instances, it would appear that pain can actually contribute to the attainment of spiritual values such as heightened sensitivity and compassion for others. Dr. Martin Luther King often spoke of the "redemptive value" of suffering, implying that much depends on the interior attitude of the one who undergoes suffering. All the same, it appears more correct to say that suffering is an evil, which faith and love can transform, with God's help, into redemptive growth.

Kinds of Evil

Various theologians and thinkers have divided the experience of evil in different ways. Perhaps the most basic and helpful distinction continues to be the difference between *natural* evil and *moral* evil.

Natural evil refers to those experiences of pain and deprivation which take place beyond the reach or influence of human freedom. This includes disasters in which natural forces bring about death or injury. Some of these, such as a bolt of lightning, may involve only one or two persons; others, such as tidal waves, drought, volcanic eruptions, and floods, may claim the lives of many thousands; still others, such as plagues and epidemics, may bring suffering and death to millions of people. Tornadoes destroy crops and damage property; hurricanes assault coastal cities; ice storms trigger automobile accidents and destroy the citrus harvest. Even as these words are being written there are millions of people dying of starvation and disease throughout the world.

As devastating as these forms of natural evil can be, there is something far more insidious and tragic about the evil that flows from human choice and sinfulness. This is usually understood as *moral* evil, since its more direct cause is the darkness of the human heart. When we focus our attention on moral evil, we come face to face with the agony which flows from human apathy, blindness of heart, or, worse still, the deliberate choice to harm other people.

The list of examples involving moral evil is long and sad: in homes there is domestic violence, child abuse, destructive conflict between spouses, sexual abuse and incest. In the wider sphere of society there are murders, rapes, muggings and gang warfare. There is white collar crime that is undetected or simply ignored. Prejudice and bigotry keep whole classes of people in oppression. Anger and hatred lead to attempts at revenge; often it is the innocent who are caught in the crossfire. There is injustice in the corrections system, which has the ironic effect of perpetuating the cycle of crime and violence. The drug trade enslaves and exploits millions; drunk drivers kill innocent people on the highways. There is pollution in our streams and in our air and chemical waste dumps in or near our cities. Whole species of wild life are being lost because of our lack of sensitivity to our environment. On the global level we have witnessed a century of war and genocide. From Auschwitz to Nagasaki we are haunted by the spectre of human destructiveness. In the meantime the build-up of nuclear weapons continues and we are faced with the ultimate form of moral evil—the destruction of human life at our own hands.

The distinction between natural and moral evil is helpful

in trying to understand the more immediate cause or origin of suffering. But we must remember that it is primarily a differentiation which we make in our minds. In the complexity and flow of life it is difficult to maintain such a distinction, since the origins and consequences of evil overlap and interpenetrate. There is, for example, an abundance of poverty, illiteracy, and malnutrition in our world. How much of this evil and the suffering which results from it is due to natural causes such as drought and famine, and how much of it depends instead on the failure of human beings to take responsibility for developing their technology in creative ways or for sharing the earth's resources in a more equitable manner? When the growing contamination of our water and food sources leads to an increase in cancer, what are we to name as the cause of this suffering? When black lung kills coal miners, or the economy puts millions of poor people out of work, how are we to assess the source or responsibility for these evils?

Obviously our reflective categories are not able to comprehend the complexity of these issues, let alone mobilize our energies and resolve to do something about them. The enormity of suffering in our world ought to be a sufficient reminder that theological thinking is a humble and limited endeavor. The distinctions which we make to understand the reality of evil are groping explorations into the realm of mystery and invitations to turn reflection into action.

The Great Dilemma

The reality of evil in the world is staggering. It can easily leave us with a sense of helplessness in the face of what appear to be destructive forces which are out of control. In some people this realization evokes an emotion of outrage and anger toward life and God. In others it induces a feeling of futility and nihilism that verges on despair. In almost everyone it raises questions. Specifically, it raises *the* question which might be described as the "Great Dilemma."

The enigma which surrounds suffering and evil has been articulated in many different ways over the centuries, depending on whether or not one had religious faith. "There's always someone playing Job," declares Mr. Zuss in Archibald MacLeish's play, *J.B.* This is a picturesque way of saying that at one time or another we all wonder about the meaning of life and especially the place of suffering and evil in the scheme of things. The Great Dilemma has been raised by believers and unbelievers alike. "Yahweh, why do you stand aside?" asks the psalmist. "Why do you hide from us now in our time of need?" (Ps 10:1). Reflecting on the circumstances of his life and times, the prophet Habakkuk poses a similar question to God: "Why do you look on while people are treacherous; why do you stay silent while the evil person oppresses the weak?" (Hab 1:13).

Later, the stoic philosopher Epicurus formulated the question in the more detached language of philosophy. As reported by the Christian Lactantius (died ca. 330), Epicurus claimed that there are only four possibilities: (1) God wants to remove evil but is unable; (2) he is able but unwilling; (3) he is neither willing nor able; (4) he is willing and able. Obviously it is the fourth option to which most people in the Judeo-Christian tradition have clung for meaning and hope. But this option does not solve the Great Dilemma. If anything, it only intensifies the difficulty: If the God we believe in is willing and able to remove evil, why hasn't this taken place? In short, how is it possible to believe in a God of love and compassion, who permits evil and suffering to have such a destructive place in our universe?

The answer which the Hebrew scriptures give to this question is ultimately one of quiet confidence in God's inscrutable ways, while continuing to question and struggle with those ways. The answer which Christianity gives, as we shall see, is the "theology of the cross" (*theologia crucis*), which only plunges us more deeply into the mystery of suffering and the vocation of compassion. The unbeliever finds neither of these to be satisfying and rejects both the Jewish and Christian traditions of faith. Perhaps John Stuart Mill, the 19th century English philosopher, puts the atheist position most succinctly and bluntly: if God is able to prevent evil and does not, then God is not good; if God would prevent evil and cannot, then God is not almighty.

The *campesinos* in the mountains of El Salvador may not be able to formulate the dilemma of pain in such precise language; but they recognize the unjust oppression which imprisons their lives, and they feel the question in their bones. The refugees of war and the victims of famine may not be able to articulate the problem of evil in philosophical language, but they still carry the "Great Why" in their hearts. It is this cry of the human heart, which transcends language and survives torture, that we must hear if we desire to enter the mystery of God. There is an old Portuguese proverb which says: "As soon as you are born, you are old enough to die." To which we might add: "And as soon as you are old enough, you begin to ask why."

[1] Three days after I completed the manuscript for this book, I received word that Keith had died. He had been in residence at the center for four and a half years. He was eleven years old when he went to God.

Questions for Reflection and Discussion

1. How has suffering touched your life and the lives of people whom you know and love? Reflect on your response to pain or loss at these times. What was your deepest emotion? Were you able to share your feelings with others? Were you open to sharing another person's pain?

2. Has the encounter with suffering or evil ever raised questions of personal meaning for you? How would you describe these questions? How did you respond to them?

3. We often speak of suffering and evil as mysteries which encompass us rather than as problems which confront us. If this is the case, what value do you think there is in seeking to understand the meaning of suffering or evil?

4. How would you describe the relationship between suffering and evil? Are they identical? Have you experienced circumstances or can you imagine circumstances in which suffering could be considered redemptive, i.e., an occasion of growth or the deepening of life's values?

Further Reading

MacLeish, Archibald, *J.B., A Play In Verse* (Boston: Houghton Mifflin, 1958).

King, Martin Luther, *Strength To Love* (New York: Pocket Books, 1968).

Paton, Alan, and others, *Creative Suffering: The Ripple of Hope* (Boston: Pilgrim Press, 1970).

Chapter 2

HOW LONG, O LORD?
Suffering and Evil in the Hebrew Scriptures

The Sound of Suffering

THE Hebrew people are more intuitive than intellectual, more in touch with the earth and less concerned about speculation for its own sake. Their language is rich in images that evoke emotion and the passion of relationships. As we begin to explore the theme of suffering in our Hebrew roots, therefore, it seems more fitting to imagine ourselves listening to the sound of voices crying out in pain, rather than thinking of suffering in conceptual terms. If it were possible to hear each cry of sorrow which has ever been uttered, it would become a mournful song of anguish almost too much for us to bear.

And yet that is the song of sorrow we would hear if we could listen to what lies behind the words of the scriptures. The Hebrew writings are as filled with the wail of pain as they are with songs of praise. Woes and disasters, diseases and defeats, give rise to a great concert of cries and complaints. In fact, weeping is so abundant in Jewish writing that it has given birth to a distinctive literary form—the *lamentation*. The sound of suffering is everywhere: the hungry cry out to Pharaoh for bread during the time of famine (Gn 41:55); the prophets raise their voices against those who perpetrate violence and oppression on the innocent. But most of all, the voice of the suffering rises directly to God. Thus the Hebrew slaves in Egypt cry out to their creator for deliverance (Ex 1:23f); and after they are freed, the sons and daughters of Israel cry out to Yahweh to be their rock and their stronghold (Ex 14:10; Jg 3:9). The psalms are a mosaic of prayer which alternates between confident praise and desperate pain.

In order to grasp more fully this sound of suffering, we might, in our imaginations, widen its scope beyond Israel to become the voice of humanity throughout the centuries: the cry of the innocent, the weeping of the children, the tears of dying soldiers, the signs of the prisoners and refugees, the silent despair of the starving and the enslaved. This litany of sorrow finds its most painful and eloquent expression in the great cry of Jesus on the cross: "My God, my God, why have you abandoned me?" (Mt 27:46; cf also Ps 22:1).

It is only when we view Jesus as the climactic expression of human suffering as well as the enfleshment of divine love that the mystery of the cross begins to take on its full significance. Jesus did not come to remove the pain of the world through a grandiose gesture of power. Rather, he chose the pathway of suffering as the only answer to the mystery of evil. In effect, Jesus became humanity's cry of anguish and God's response of compassion. "During the days of his flesh," writes the author of Hebrews, "Jesus offered up prayer and entreaty, aloud and in silent tears, to the one who had the power to save him out of death . . ." (He 5:7).

Later we shall discuss the deeper implications of Jesus' suffering and death. For now it is enough that we place the Hebrew understanding of suffering and evil within this realistic setting of humanity's cry of sorrow.

The Seriousness of Suffering

The reality of suffering and evil is difficult to deny, since it confronts us almost daily in some form or another. But there are different ways that people can choose to respond to this reality. One person might become withdrawn and isolated; another might engage in emotional denial. Some individuals respond to pain with anger and rebellion. Others try to bargain their way out of suffering with prayer and promises. Finally, some choose to enter the experience with quiet trust, accepting the fact that pain is indeed a reality in their lives, but relying on God for the strength to keep on going. Denial, anger, bargaining, depression, acceptance: according to Elisabeth Kubler-Ross, we pass through some or all of these stages in our attempt to come to grips with suffering and death in our lives.

This variety of personal responses to suffering can also serve as a model for understanding collective attitudes toward the reality of pain. When projected onto the larger experience of a tribe or ethnic group, they become the philosophical/theological stance of an entire people or culture. Thus, some religions are more stoical and passive in the face of pain. Others approach it as an illusory dimension of a world that is passing away, and summon their followers to move beyond sorrow to the permanent realities of the immaterial world. There is also a long religious and philosophical tradition of rebellion in the face of evil. And there is, of course, a spirituality of quiet trust and patience in the face of suffering.

What is the fundamental stance of the Hebrew tradition toward suffering and evil? A simple answer to this question is not possible, but we can establish some important parameters nevertheless. It is clear, for example, that the Hebrew mind does not approach suffering stoically. In the Jewish writings there is a presumption that suffering is an evil which ought not to be; something deep in the human heart cries out against it. The Israelites recognized the universality of suffering (cf. Jb 14:1), but they were not resigned to it. They believed that wisdom and good health should go together as gifts from God.

In simple terms, the bible does not enjoy suffering. It praises the doctor as an instrument of healing (Si 38:1f); it awaits the messianic era as a time of healing the hurts of life. Here and there we find hints of victory over death and even the hope of resurrection (cf Is 26:19; Jb 19:23-27). In the practical sphere, the Hebrew writings call upon the community to reach out to the widows, the orphans, and the strangers to help alleviate their pain. For the Jewish person, in short, suffering was a reality to be faced, to be wrestled with, cried out against, and alleviated wherever and whenever possible.

The Scandal of Suffering

The religion of Israel came into being in the setting of a major historical event: the exodus from Egypt to the promised land. It was in the process of this saving journey that the Hebrew people came to know God as their savior and liberator. It was in the desert that the covenant was born and Israel became a believing people. But the crucible in which their faith came to painful maturity was not the desert, but Palestine surrounded by the Canaanite cultures and the earthy attraction of pagan practices. The nations which surrounded Israel and influenced its cultural attitudes were, for the most part, polytheistic in their belief systems.

This had several implications, not least of which was a radically different way of working out the problem of evil. The Canaanite religions attempted to explain the mystery of suffering and evil on the basis of various quarrels or tensions among the gods. This is but one of many dualist ways of resolving the issue of evil in the world. It allows people to blame the painful times on evil gods and to rejoice in the prosperous times as gifts from the good gods. Thus Mot, the Canaanite god of death, becomes the dumping ground for all the evils and pain of the world; and Baal, with his consort Astarte, is envisioned as the source of life, joy, and the return of spring each year.

At first this may appear to be an oversimplified way of looking at things, but it is also a rather attractive solution to the Great Dilemma. It places the origin of evil outside the natural sphere, and provides a framework within which people can resign themselves to the whims of the gods or the cosmic fates of the universe. It also becomes a convenient way to shrug off any human responsibility for evil in the world. The dualist approach is ancient and enduring. There are millions of religious people in our world who view the mystery of suffering through these theological lenses.

This, however, was not an acceptable solution for the Hebrew people. Israel's faith was based not on many gods, but on the One God, Yahweh. "Listen, Israel," goes the Shema, "Yahweh is our God, Yahweh alone" (Dt 6:4). In the monotheism of Israel, the one God must somehow be the source of both the good and the bad in creation. The dilemma of faith which this created for the Israelites was no small matter. Perhaps that is why they often found themselves so attracted to the pagan belief system and the earthy practices of their neighbors.

This temptation became even stronger during the time of the exile. With their dreams broken and the promises of Yahweh seemingly forgotten, it was relatively easy for them to believe that Yahweh had been conquered by more powerful gods. More than once the Israelite people gave in to this temptation to deny their relationship with the transcendent God of Abraham, Isaac, and Jacob, and turned instead to the ways of their pagan neighbors. They went often to the "high places," the sanctuaries of the Canaanites, and entered into the earthy rhythm of their worship.

It is precisely this practice of adopting pagan forms of worship which the prophets denounced as a fundamental betrayal of the covenant with Yahweh. What is significant, however, is that even as they excoriated the people for committing "adultery" by turning their backs on their relationship with God, the prophets never tried to make excuses for God in the face of suffering and evil. If there is one God then the mystery of pain must somehow be traced back to this divine origin of life. Instead of excusing their creator and redeemer the prophets argue that suffering does not escape God's notice. "I fashion the light and create the darkness," Isaiah says on behalf of God. "I make happiness and I cause misery" (Is 45:7). This may appear at first glance to be as unnuanced as the belief of Israel's neighbors, but it is profoundly consistent with monotheism. The Israelite tradition never abandons the bold vision articulated by Amos: "Does misfortune come to a city if Yahweh has not sent it?" (Am 3:6).

This faithfulness to the monotheistic vision comes only at the price of wrestling with the mystery of pain at a deeper level. If evil and suffering are under the providence of God, then Israel faces an even more powerful enigma. What kind of God is this which allows and, in some mysterious way, causes suffering? The poets of Israel knew the implications of such a stance and the deep waters to which it might lead. The wicked, when faced with evil in the world, will only find confirmation that "there is no God!" (Ps 10:4; 14:1). Others will conclude that if God does exist it must be a God "incapable of knowledge" (Ps 73:11). The wife of Job pushes the argument to its final desperate conclusion: she advises her beleaguered husband to "curse God" (Jb 2:9).

The Israelites took suffering seriously—so seriously that they confronted it as a scandal of faith, an enigma in the heart of life that can neither be ignored, philosophically explained, or patiently accepted. They rebelled against suffering even as they clung to God in the dark night of faith.

Early Explanations of Suffering and Evil

At the same time that the Israelites wrestled with the meaning of suffering and its relationship to God, they also explored various intermediate causes. For the most part these explanations for evil and human sorrow are rooted in the commonsense wisdom which the Hebrews handed on from generation to generation. We can also detect the influence of cultures which surrounded Israel.

1) *The Rhythm of Nature.* Some of the pain of life arises from its natural cycles: the coming and going of the seasons, the ebb and flow of life's energy. The Hebrews were an earthy people, so they understood both the beauty and the terror of nature's ways. In early Judaism there was no developed doctrine of an after-life, so the richness of life and the fragility of its gifts had to be cherished in the limited span of a lifetime. Hebrew realism embraced life's blessings and its burdens with an amazing openness. It recognized that much of life's fragility arises from the limits of the physical world. When the story of Jacob and Esau is told, for instance, an essential element of the drama is the fact that Isaac has grown old and his eyes are so weak that he can no longer see adequately (Gn 27:1). Likewise the author of II Samuel points out that Saul's grandson was crippled as a young child, when his nurse accidentally dropped him at a time of crisis and haste, thus maiming him for life.

In the familiar description of Qoheleth, "There is a season for everything, and a time for every occupation under heaven (Qo 3:1). In addition to the storms, famines, and other unwanted experiences in nature, there is the steady unfolding of life. We are born, we grow up, and we grow old. One of life's simple truths is that nature takes its toll.

2) *Evil Powers.* The rhythms of nature, even in their most unexpected fury, cannot account for the evil which appears to be in control of human life. Thus the Hebrew people, like many of their near-eastern neighbors, developed a belief in super-human powers, which, they believed, held the world and its inhabitants under their sway.

This portrait of malevolent spiritual beings comes to light only gradually in the history of revelation. What were the origins of this perspective? It should not surprise us that the Israelites, like most ethnic and religious groups in history, were influenced by the cultures which surrounded them. The ancient Orient bestowed personalities on the myriads of obscure forces which they could not understand or explain. The next step was to assign the host of unexplained evils which assail the human race to these same obscure forces.

We have historical evidence that the Babylonian religions had developed a rather intricate form of demonology, in which several forms of exorcism were practiced to deliver bewitched persons, things, and places. Basically these were rites of magic which were part of medical practice, since most sicknesses were attributed to the action of an evil spirit. Even though the Israelites respected the normal processes of nature, including sickness, they also acknowledged the presence of malevolent spirits. The Hebrew scriptures frequently employ the folklore of the time to explain terrifying encounters with evil (cf Is 13:21; 34:12,14; Lv 16:10; Ps 91:6; Dt 32:24).

In some instances the fear of superhuman evil came to be identified with "the Curse"—a conviction that at some point in history an act of rebellion had occurred which triggered a mysterious retaliation of evil forces. In addition, the Hebrews believed that the spoken word carried the powerful capacity of releasing these evil forces with a kind of deadly inexorability. A curse is like the reverse echo of the creative Word of God. In the beginning there was the blessing of God's self-communication in creation. When God speaks there is an overflow of life and graciousness.

In contrast, the Tempter, who defies God, draws human beings into sin and into the curse of evil. As a result, the "original blessing" is ruptured and exile and death follow.

In the history of Hebrew thought the world of evil spirits gradually came to be identified with Satan. In Hebrew the term "Satan" carries the meaning of "the enemy" or "the adversary;" in Greek the term is *diabolos*—the devil, which is more correctly translated as "the slanderer" or "the liar." In contrast to the majority of the cultures in the Near East, the Hebrew bible speaks of Satan only rarely and then in a manner which carefully preserves the transcendence of God and avoids the prevalent temptation to see evil as a rival to Yahweh (as in the earliest forms of dualism).

In fact, Satan is pictured as one of the angels in the court of Yahweh. His role might be compared to that of a public prosecutor who is entrusted with insuring respect on earth for the justice and rights of God. This is the profile of Satan that we are given in the opening scenes of the Book of Job. But beneath his pretended service of God, there are already signs of hostility and a mind bent on disruption and alienation. It is this mysterious figure which the poets of Israel eventually identify with the Tempter in the garden (Gn 3:1). It is this same presence of evil which Jesus will name as "the murderer and liar from the beginning" (Jn 8:44).

3) *Human Sinfulness.* As we have seen, many near-eastern cultures resolved the problem of suffering by believing in an evil god which stood in fundamental conflict with the benevolent divinity. The effect of this was to relieve human beings of their role in the problem of evil. The Hebrew tra-

dition does not follow this trajectory of thought. They place the emergence of evil in the world squarely on the shoulders of human beings who freely turn from God when tempted by the evil one.

In the early stages of Hebrew thinking there was a somewhat simplistic tendency to look for a human fault behind every woe. We can study an example of this approach in Psalm 1, which assumes that there are two roads which a human person can walk: the path of evil or the way of life. We are also assured by the psalmist that our choices will have direct consequences for our happiness: "Yahweh takes care of the way the virtuous go, but the way of the wicked is doomed" (Ps 1:6). Ironically, this is precisely the presumption of Job's friends, who insist that evil doesn't just happen in someone's life; he must be guilty of some wrong-doing before God.

The Scandal of Suffering and Biblical Questioning

For several centuries the explanations for suffering which we have just summarized (the cycle of nature, evil spirits, and human sinfulness) continued to play a significant role in Israel's confrontation with the reality of evil. As time went on, however, it became increasingly clear that they raised as many questions as they answered. Why would a loving God fashion a world in which suffering was a normal part of life? Why did the God of Israel allow the evil ones such latitude in the course of human affairs? And most importantly, how are we to comprehend the meaning of innocent, good people who are burdened with suffering?

Somewhere between the 6th and 4th centuries B.C.E. an

important transformation in the Jewish theology of suffering began to take shape. It was initiated by the ongoing quest of the prophets to understand the ways of Yahweh. In prayer and in their preaching they realized that the usual explanations for suffering were at best stumbling attempts to find causes in the world of common sense. But the mystery of suffering could no longer be contained by the limited parameters of the early wisdom teachings. In their hearts the prophets knew that neither nature nor chance, neither the fatal offspring of sin nor the curse, nor even Satan himself falls outside the power of God. The questions and the searching kept leading them back to God.

Soon they began to challenge the oversimplifications of the early wisdom literature and the proverbial sayings of the people. Again and again they express their dismay at the prosperity of the wicked and the misery of the just (cf Jr 12: 1-6; Ha 1:13; 3:14-18). The prophet Ezechiel is one of the first to attack the widespread assumption that suffering is the delayed consequences of our ancestors' sins.

This spirit of biblical questioning became even more pronounced in the later wisdom writings, in what many scholars refer to as the "literature of revolt." This body of writing includes the poetic reflections of Job and Qoheleth, which, though they are classified under the general heading of wisdom literature, are nevertheless part of a rebellion against the early simplistic solutions to suffering.

Job: The Suffering of the Just

The story of Job is the classic biblical formulation of the problem of evil. It is a literary masterpiece written in post-exilic times (probably the beginning of the 5th century, B.C.E.), when Israel's concern with the destiny of the nation as a whole was shifting toward a preoccupation with the individual and the meaning of personal life.

The book opens with a prose narrative which sets forth the dilemma of a prosperous, faithful man whose life steadily disintegrates. God allows Satan to test him to see if he will remain faithful despite misfortune.

The main body of the book is a long dialogue poem in which Job and his three friends argue about the meaning of divine justice and human life. The author uses the three friends as a poetic framework within which to articulate the traditional thesis of earthly retribution: the good are rewarded and the evil are punished in this life. They offer the familiar explanations for the presence of evil: (1) the happiness of the wicked is only temporary; (2) the suffering of good people is God's way of testing their fortitude; (3) the sufferings of the just are punishment for faults which have been committed unwittingly or out of weakness. The issue is simple: if Job is suffering, it is because he has sinned. When Job protests his innocence, the three only become more obstinate. Later in the poem a third figure, Elihu, appears and develops the traditional arguments further.

In the meantime Job reflects on his own experience. Out of the depth of his anguish he pleads his cause. He confronts the traditional theories with the justice of his life and the widespread experience of injustice in the world. He takes his questions and his protest all the way to God and demands an answer. In effect God's response is that there is no answer, since the wisdom and mystery of the divine is beyond the human capacity to understand.

The book ends with an epilogue in prose, in which God rebukes the three friends, rewards Job with children, and doubles his possessions. Many scholars are convinced that this ending is actually a later supplement to the original poetic piece, an addition which ironically reflects the need for "a happy ending" and falls back into the framework of the earlier theories of retribution. The heart of the story is clearly Job's encounter with God and his acceptance of mystery. The message of the Book of Job is actually disarmingly simple: faith must carry on even when understanding fails. This is as far as the author can take the issue of suffering at this stage in the history of revelation.

Qoheleth, the Questioner

Qoheleth is sometimes called the "existentialist" of the Hebrew bible. Instead of evading the painful questions of life or dismissing them with pious proverbs, "The Preacher" (the literal translation of the Hebrew word "Qoheleth") names the ambiguity and paradox which is at the center of human existence. Writing after the exile, the author puts words to the feelings of futility and emptiness which permeate the daily routine of people, even those who believe in a loving and provident God.

Qoheleth's question is the same as Job's: do virtue and vice get their just deserts on earth? Does it make any difference in terms of outward success if I am a good and upright person? Both Job and Qoheleth give the same answer to this question: No, it does not. Unlike Job, who seeks for answers in the midst of his pain, Qoheleth is actually enjoying good health. He discovers that happiness itself is an illusory, empty thing. Qoheleth seems to be saying that we must simply accept life as it is, with its limited joys and its abundant enigmas. The ways of God will always be a puzzle to human beings, but God has no need to justify them to us. In the midst of it all Qoheleth maintains his faith in God.

Entering the Mystery of Suffering

In one of his letters, the poet Rainier Rilke speaks of the importance of "living the questions" of life, implying that the human quest takes us beyond solutions and explanations into the mystery itself. In a sense this is what Israel as a whole and the authors of the "literature of revolt" were doing in the centuries following the exile. They knew that common sense could not explain suffering. They recognized that the traditional proverbs regarding God's justice did not square with their experience. They realized, in short, that they had run out of answers. It was time to raise new questions and to confront the paradox at a deeper level. This was precisely the role of Job and Qoheleth; the genius of their faith was to transform the horizon of suffering and to risk taking it directly to God. The answer to suffering is that there is no answer. Beyond our questions there is only trust in God.

But trust and faith are not solutions; they are invitations toward a relationship and a journey. They are challenges to "live the questions"—to walk into the darkness of suffering in the hope of finding meaning by embracing it. In Psalm 73 the poet recalls the ways in which he has been haunted by life's paradoxes and describes his frustration with the search for answers "until the day I *entered the mystery*" (Ps 73:17, italics mine). The next stage in the quest to understand the meaning of evil and pain is contained in this image of "entering the mystery," not in search of rational answers but in the hope of encountering God.

At about the same time that Job and Qoheleth were being written, we also find another biblical perspective coming into being which explores suffering as redemptive service and as an act of healing love. When Israel looked back over its history it could see that even in the darkest of times, when the covenantal promises seemed empty and when hope appeared to be gone, Yahweh—God—stayed with them and carried them toward life.

The classic instance of God's faithfulness in the midst of alienation is found in the story of Joseph. After the patriarch Jacob dies, the brothers of Joseph come to him recognizing the evil they have done and the pain they have inflicted on him unjustly. They beg his forgiveness and tell him that they are prepared to be his slaves. But Joseph replies: "Do not be afraid; is it for me to put myself in God's place? The evil you planned to do to me has by God's design been turned to good, that he might bring about, as indeed he has, the deliverance of a numerous people" (Gn 50:19-20). What is striking about Joseph's reply is that it furnishes no answer or explanation of evil; it only points to the need for trusting in God's redemptive presence. Nothing can prevent God's love from bringing forth life, not even the suffering that flows from human sin and selfishness.

The Servant: Redemptive Suffering

Perhaps the most mysterious and striking figure in the sacred writings of the Hebrews is that of the Servant (in Hebrew, *ebed,* which literally means "slave") which appears in four poems or songs in Isaiah 40-55. It is this figure which most powerfully embodies the understanding of suffering as redemptive of sin and separation. The scholarly debate still continues regarding the identity and role of this servant figure. What matters for our purposes, however, is the vision and experience of suffering which the servant, whatever his identity, offers to the history of revelation.

In one respect the Servant is portrayed as a prophet: he is endowed with the Spirit (42:1); he speaks out, but he does not shout (42:2; 49:2); he is sent to teach the nations (50:4). On the other hand, he also has many qualities of a king: he brings forth judgment (42:3f) and he is a light and a medium of salvation (49:6) to the nations. Perhaps the author of these poems has chosen the title "Servant" to indicate that he is speaking of someone whose life goes beyond the role of prophet and king, even beyond a Second Moses, indeed beyond anything which we have yet heard or seen in a leader. The work of the Servant reaches its climax in the Fourth Song (52:13-53:12). In this poem the Servant is described as fulfilling a role that no other charismatic figure in Israel has taken. He freely chooses to make himself a sin offering for the people. He heals others through his innocent suffering and brings about justice and peace, not through his conquests, but by giving his blood for others.

The Servant's answer to the pain and brokenness of the world is to take it upon himself and carry it in love. Instead of trying to achieve justice through human argument or retribution, the Servant "enters the mystery" and embraces suffering as the way toward redemption. "He was pierced through for our faults, crushed for our sins. On him lies a punishment that brings us peace, and through his wounds we are healed" (53:5).

It is not an exaggeration to say that the Servant figure represents the climax of Israel's struggle with the mystery of suffering and evil. The *ebed Yahweh* is a vision and a presence which points beyond itself to a redemptive act which only God can accomplish. As we know from the Christian scriptures, the Servant is the figure with which Jesus identifies his life and ministry. The Isaiahan poems become one of the richest sources for the early church to understand and interpret the redemptive meaning of Jesus' death and resurrection.

Questions for Reflection/Discussion

1. Discuss the meaning of "lamentation" in the Hebrew scriptures and in the life of prayer. In your opinion is "complaint" a less noble form of prayer than praise or thanksgiving? Why or why not? Have you ever complained to God in prayer? Under what circumstances?

2. Do you have a characteristic response to pain (e.g. denial, anger, bargaining, depression, acceptance, etc.)? Or do you find that you move through different emotional and spiritual "phases" when faced with suffering in yourself or others? If so, what are these emotional/ spiritual stages for you?

3. Why was the reality of evil and suffering more problematic for the Israelites than for the cultures which surrounded them? In what sense were evil and human anguish a "scandal" for the Hebrew believer? Is it similarly a "scandal" for you?

4. What is your response to the early explanations of evil among the Hebrews? Discuss your ideas regarding evil spirits or the devil as the source of evil and suffering in the world.

5. The early wisdom tradition believed that suffering was a direct result of personal sinfulness. What is your evaluation of this perspective? Do you know people or groups who explicitly or implicitly hold this view today?

6. In what context did the "questioning" tradition in Israel arise? What is your response to Job and Qoheleth? Can you identify aspects of your own experience with their questions? In what way?

Further Reading

Brown, Fitzmyer, & Murphy, eds., *The Jerome Biblical Commentary* (Englewood Cliffs, NJ: Prentice Hall, 1968).

Bergant, Diane, C.S.A., *Job, Ecclesiates,* Vol. 18 in *The Old Testament Message* (Wilmington: Michael Glazier, 1982).

Kubler-Ross, Elisabeth, *On Death And Dying* (New York: MacMillan Co., 1969).

Leon-Dufour, Xavier, S. J., *Dictionary of Biblical Theology* (New York: Desclee Co., 1967).

Murphy, Roland E., *The Psalms, Job* in *The Proclamation Commentaries* (Philadelphia: Fortress Press, 1977).

Chapter 3

I AM THE WAY
Jesus and the Mystery of Evil

A FEW years ago there was a bumper sticker which read: "Jesus is the answer!" As a popular way of proclaiming faith in Christ this advertisement may have had a certain validity. After all, Jesus did proclaim some rather clear principles regarding our ethical and religious lives. He worked miracles that astounded the crowds; he healed many of the sick, the lame, and the blind. According to the gospels he also raised at least two people from the dead and promised to give eternal life to all who believed in him. He assured his followers that if they put their trust in him, he would give them the Spirit of truth to enlighten their minds and hearts.

Does that mean that Jesus is the answer? In the deepest sense, yes. But given the proclivity of human beings to seek for or demand simplistic answers for complex issues, the bumper sticker and the stance behind it leave something to be desired.

In the first place, it is remarkable how rarely Jesus gives direct replies to people who are looking for black and white answers. Usually Jesus responds to their questions with a query of his own, or he tells them a story and then asks them to interpret it or apply it. A striking example of this teaching method occurs in the famous parable of the Good Samaritan (Lk 10:25-37). A lawyer came to Jesus with a question: "What must I do to inherit eternal life?" A simple enough question which seems to invite a direct reply. Instead, Jesus returns the question: "What is written in the Law? What do you read there?" When the lawyer quotes the Great Commandment of love, Jesus affirms this response and invites the lawyer to live by it. But the lawyer presses the point further: "And who is my neighbor?" Another simple question, inviting another simple answer. This time Jesus responds with the story of the Good Samaritan and ends with another question: "Which of these three, in your opinion, was neighbor to the man?"

What is implied in Jesus's manner of responding to people's questions and concerns? What is Jesus trying to teach us about human life? It appears from interactions like the one described above that Jesus does not intend to furnish answers to religious issues in any simplistic manner. If anything, he invites people to find the answers to life's great questions in their hearts and through the choices which they are challenged to make regarding the reign of God. In short, Jesus approached life and people with a profound reverence for their dignity and mystery. Jesus did not say: "I am the answer;" he did say, "I am the way . . ." (Jn 14:6). Jesus seems to imply that the only answer to the ultimate questions is to follow him into life, to live his journey and to embrace his way.

This is especially true when it comes to the question of suffering and the meaning of evil. The only answer Jesus gives to suffering and evil is the gift of his life. No one has ever entered the mystery of pain as deeply and as generously as he did.

The Great Struggle

From beginning to end the public ministry of Jesus is the story of a warfare between the hostile powers of evil and

the graciousness of a loving God. It is not without irony
that the first voice to recognize the identity and mission of
Jesus in Mark's gospel is that of an evil spirit. When Jesus
enters the synagogue in Capernaum he encounters a man
with an unclean spirit which cries out: "What have you to
do with us, Jesus of Nazareth? Have you come to destroy
us? I know who you are, the Holy One of God" (Mk 1:24).
The people in need of healing love are everywhere, but the
first presence to recognize his true identity and mission is
that of the evil one.

According to the evangelists this combat with evil had
begun even before Jesus began his public ministry. Each of
the gospels opens with an account of Jesus' encounter with
the evil one in the desert. Most exegetes agree that the
temptation accounts are probably stylized summaries of a
testing which continued in one form or another throughout
the public ministry of Jesus. It was as though he must first
confront the dark forces in the desert of his own life before
he could achieve the work of redemption in the world. The
message of the evangelists is clear: where Israel chose the
pathway of resistance and hardheartedness in the desert,
Jesus, the New Israel, overcomes darkness and inaugurates
the final exodus—the Easter Passover which will lead to
new life.

Casting Out Demons

In the gospel accounts there are several episodes in
which Jesus casts out demons. As we study these events, it
is important to remember the distinctive understanding
which the people of that time had regarding the demonic.

They attributed directly to evil spirits certain phenomena which today would probably fall in the category of psychiatry or other areas of medicine. This is in no way to deny what are clear instances of possession (e.g. Mk 1:23f;5:6), but only to point out that in many cases diabolic possession and physical/emotional illness were intermingled. In the popular mind of the day every sickness was understood to be a confirmation of Satan's power over human life.

How are we to interpret the exorcism stories in light of this cultural and religious background? These miracles are intended by Jesus to be *signs*—powerful indicators that the God of life is confronting and conquering the kingdom of death. The language which the evangelists employ assists us in gaining deeper insight into the meaning of these individual victories over Satan. Sometimes Jesus is said to heal the possessed (Lk 6:18; 7:21). At other times he drives out or casts out evil spirits (Mk 1:34-39). The ministry of Jesus is "parabolic;" that is, it speaks of a deeper reality which is going on in the cosmos. In the view of the evangelists, whenever Jesus confronts sickness, he is confronting Satan. Whenever he heals, Jesus triumphs over the powers of evil.

Deeper Forms of Evil

It is not just in the lives of individuals that Jesus struggles with evil. He also names the demons which are embodied in the social and religious institutions of his age. Jesus confronts the evil which he finds in the political and military occupation of Palestine by the Romans. He speaks out against the juridical oppression which is embodied in many aspects of the Jewish religion. Later on Paul would speak of these forms of institutional violence as "the principalities and the powers"—the evil which permeates the institutions of society and the structures of the cosmos because of human sin and brokenness. The "principalities and the powers" is an image for the deeper mystery of evil which goes beyond our personal comprehension and control. A single individual is not responsible for imagining or creating a Dachau or an Auschwitz. Similarly, we would be hard pressed to find any one who actually wants to destroy the world in a nuclear holocaust. And yet, the truth remains that there are Auschwitzs in this world, and even now humanity stands at the brink of that which, as individuals, we speak of as the unthinkable.

We are left to wonder about our human helplessness. How can things get so out of hand? Why is there so much evil when there are so many good-willed people? We can blame much of the world's brokenness on personal sin and exploitation: but there is something more, some unspoken and terrifying expansion of sin that seems beyond our imagination and control.

In the end, it was this deeper, collective mystery of evil which brought about the death of Jesus. It was not because he cast out evil spirits in the lives of individuals or because he reached out to the physically and economically oppressed that Jesus went to Golgotha. A few marginated people brought to wholeness in a remote part of the Roman empire would have caused only a minor stir among the curious and the powerful. But Jesus did not limit his confrontation with evil to the lives of individuals. He named the demons in the political and religious structures of his age as well. He touched the raw nerve of "respectable power''—evil that has taken on the guise of legitimacy because it is finely clothed and camouflaged by respect or fear. Jesus went to his death, according to the Latin American theologian Juan Mateos, because he named the demons of "claiming" (greed), "controlling" (dominative power), and "climbing" (the lust for fame) in the political and religious structures of his time.

The reality of evil is more enormous and frightening than our human minds can comprehend. In the presence of such a mystery our words become inadequate and empty. Jesus may indeed be the "answer" as the bumper sticker announces, but it is an answer which leads us into the heart of darkness in the quest for light.

The Response of Jesus to Suffering

What did Jesus do for people who were in pain? What was his emotional response to the reality of suffering? What do his preaching and ministry tell us about God's compassion? Finally, what meaning is there for us in the agony and death of Jesus and his resurrection to new life?

Jesus of Nazareth was born into a religious tradition which loved life and cherished the goodness of the earth. His temperament and his world-view were rooted in the Hebraic response to the joys and the enigmas of daily living. We cannot hope to grasp his approach to evil if we do not respect his religious and cultural heritage. If there is a characteristic quality about Jesus' relationship to people and life, it is probably that of *involvement*—an intense engagement and participation in the energy of life.

This love for life becomes all the more striking when we contrast Jesus' response to pain and death with that of some of the other great figures in history. It is fascinating, for instance, to compare Jesus and Socrates as each of them confronted his approaching death. By any standard both of them are heroic figures who are considered martyrs for the values which shaped their lives. But there the likeness ends. On the night before his death, Socrates is portrayed as gathering his friends together for a symposium supper, at which he dispassionately speaks of the value of dying as an escape from the body and the world of passing shadows. He chides his friends for their feelings of grief and calmly drinks the hemlock.

Jesus, on the other hand, approaches his hour with fear and dread, even as he continues to trust in his Father. He gathers his friends for a last meal, gives them an example of loving service, and speaks of the hour of darkness. He then takes his closest friends apart in the garden, begs them to stay awake with him, and enters into a time of inner agony, as he pleads with God to deliver him from the jaws of death. In the perspective of Greek philosophy this would have been looked upon as a cowardly response. In the tradition of Hebraic belief and humanness, however, it is the story of a just man who cherishes life and who enters fully into the mystery of suffering. In other words, Jesus does not view suffering as an illusion or death as an escape. As a Jew he responds to suffering and death as realities that must be wrestled with, not just intellectually, but with one's total self.

We cannot limit Jesus' encounter with suffering to his passion and death. Long before Gethsemani and Golgotha he had already begun to drink the cup of sorrow. Jesus knew the pain of rejection from his own people (cf Jn

1:11); he was misunderstood by his disciples and hated by
the religious authorities of Israel; he wept over Jerusalem
(Lk 19:41); and, from the point of view of human feelings,
he watched his dreams of proclaiming the reign of God
crumble in the dust.

Because Jesus was a man "familiar with suffering" (Is
53:3), he was also sensitive to the pain of other people. The
evangelists describe the response of Jesus to suffering in
images that reveal the depth of his humanness and compassion.

1) Anger. The inadequacy of translations and the innate
suspicion of emotion in Western culture tend to conceal
the fact that Jesus responded to evil with anger. This is
particularly true in the gospel of Mark, where the author
retains a more straightforward description of feelings.
When a leper approaches Jesus and begs for healing, Mark
indicates that Jesus' first response was anger (Mk 3:5-6).
The word in Greek (*splagnizomai*) is often translated as
"feeling sorry for" or "having pity towards," but more
accurately it implies an intense anger toward the presence
of suffering—an anger which flows over into compassion
toward the person who is inflicted by it.

The anger of Jesus also flares up in the face of hypocrisy
and the evil of religious legalism. Again, Mark gives us
the most graphic example of this (Mk 3:1-6). Jesus encounters a man with a withered hand in a local synagogue
and is aware that the religious leaders are watching to see if
he will heal on the sabbath. Mark gives us this account of
what transpired: "Then Jesus said to them, 'Is it against
the law on the sabbath day to do good, or to do evil; to

save life, or to kill?' But they said nothing. Then, *grieved* to find them so obstinate, he looked *angrily* round at them, and said to the man, 'Stretch out your hand.' He stretched it out and his hand was better'' (italics mine).

This is the same anger that consumes Jesus when he drives the sellers and buyers from the temple. This is not only an instance of prophetic zeal, but of authentic rage in the face of evil and the oppression of God's "little ones."

2) *Compassion.* In the ancient Hebrew the word for compassion has the same root as the term for "womb," implying that the attitude of reaching out to suffering people can only be compared to a mother's love for her child. Jesus is the human face of God's seeking love and care, the embodiment of divine compassion. The gospel narratives abound with scenes which portray Jesus as being moved by the suffering of the people: "When he saw the crowds his heart was moved with compassion, because they were harassed and dejected, like sheep without a shepherd" (cf also Mt 14:14; 15:32; Lk 7:13; 15:20).

The opposite of compassion is not hatred but apathy —the refusal to be moved to pity and to action in the face of relievable human suffering. Apathy is another word for what Jesus refers to as "blindness of heart"—the refusal to see God in the midst of life, especially in the needs of others, and to respond to those needs with love. Here is another instance where Jesus reverses the cultural sensitivities of his age. The self-righteous leaders of Judaism found it easy to categorize people into classes of sinners such as the "prostitutes and tax collectors," while maintaining an aura of moral superiority among themselves.

Jesus, on the other hand, is compassionate toward the sinners because he sees them as hungry for the kingdom and willing to be converted. Their brokenness does not provoke his anger but his caring. It is precisely the aloofness and hypocrisy of the religious leaders which Jesus names as the real sin of his age. It is because they have chosen to be "blind of heart" that they will be condemned.

3) *Helplessness.* There are moments of victory in the public ministry of Jesus. He successfully casts out demons and heals many people of their disease and isolation. He sends forth the twelve and the seventy-two with the power to extend his work of conquering evil and freeing people to embrace the reign of God. When the disciples return from their first journey, they are exuberant with joy and tell Jesus in amazement that "the devils submit to us when we use your name" (Lk 10:17). Affirming their confidence, Jesus tells them: "I watched Satan fall like lightening from heaven. Yes, I have given you power to tread underfoot serpents and scorpions and the whole strength of the enemy; nothing shall ever hurt you. Yet do not rejoice that the spirits submit to you; rejoice rather that your names are written in heaven" (Lk 10:18-20).

If we were to read these and similar passages in isolation, we might conclude that the victory over evil will be total and relatively easy. The rest of the gospel, however, tells a different story. There will indeed be a victory, but it will not be along the lines that we might humanly expect or want. Paradoxically, the final victory over evil comes not through powerful exorcisms or miraculous healings, not through human achievement, but through divine helpless-

ness. Redemption takes place through the free choice of
Jesus to fulfill the role of the Servant figure in Isaiah. He
conquers evil by first becoming its victim.

Jesus: God's Answer to Suffering

If we gathered all the healing and exorcism stories of the
gospel and multiplied them ten-fold, it would still represent only a tiny fraction of the suffering people who lived
in Palestine at the time. It would include an even smaller
fraction of the vast multitudes that have carried pain in
their lives during the centuries before and after Christ. If
the purpose of Jesus' ministry was to cast out all forms of
evil, to heal all physical and emotional suffering, and to
take away the pain of death, we can only conclude that he
failed.

Even in the two instances in which Jesus actually raised
people from the dead, it was not a definitive conquering of
death as an event in human life. The widow of Naim was
consoled by having back her only son, but we can assume
that at some point the young man grew old or ill and faced
that dark mystery again. The same is true of Lazarus. Jesus
wept at the death of his dear friend and then called him
forth from the tomb. But there is no indication that
Lazarus thereby became exempt from mortality or any
other dimension of the human condition. Perhaps the most
poignant words in the Lazarus story are those of the
mourner who asks: "Could he (Jesus) not have done
something to keep this man from dying?" (Jn 11:36). Yes,
of course he could do something, we might be tempted to
reply; he is, after all, the Son of God. If it were only a

question of power perhaps the work of redemption would be more understandable to us.

But the mystery only deepens: whether or not he *could* do something to keep Lazarus or any one else from dying, the fact is that Jesus did *not* do anything to prevent us from experiencing death. The only answer which is given to the mourner is Jesus' willingness to enter into death himself. Ironically, we can raise the same question regarding Jesus: Could God not have done something to keep this man from dying? The only answer is the immense love which rendered God "helpless" in the face of Jesus' passion and death. The divine power did not intervene to rescue Jesus or to "fix" human pain by an act of heavenly magic. "God loved the world so much," John tells us, "that he gave his only Son" (Jn 3:16).

Jesus is not the kind of "answer" to pain that popular religion would propose. He redeemed humanity, but he did not remove suffering or death. He worked miracles only as signs of the deeper victory which he believed God would bring about in the kingdom. Jesus did not suppress human anguish; he consoled those who experienced it and then took it upon himself. He did not abolish tears; he only dried some of them while passing by (Lk 7:13), as a promise of the joy that will blossom forth when God "will wipe away the tears from all eyes" (Ap 21:4).

If Jesus did not come to eradicate suffering and death, then how can we call him savior? If the paradox and ambiguity of human life still remain, in what sense is Jesus the "Kyrios" (Lord)—conqueror of evil and darkness?

The Christian gospel invites us to believe in a God of unconditional love, who cares so deeply for creation and the pain of people that the divine unites itself with the human. God's response to evil is to confront it in the humanity of Jesus, to carry it in humble service, to struggle against it with intense human rage, to respond to the suffering masses with compassion, to experience pain to the depths, to be broken by it in the scandal of the cross, and finally to break the grip of death through the resurrection.

The Suffering of Christians

In our creeds and doctrines we proclaim this way of redemptive suffering. In our prayer and liturgy we affirm the manner in which God has loved us in Jesus and we commit ourselves in turn to live out the same pattern in our lives. But if history is any indication, we have found it easier to speak the words than to live the mystery. The temptation to escape from the human condition still haunts us. The suffering of Jesus appears to be as much a "scandal" to us as it was for Simon Peter (Mk 8:32). In times of doubt or struggle the cross seems more of an "absurdity" (I Cor 1:23-34) than an instrument which transforms the meaning of suffering. Why couldn't God, who is all-powerful, have found a more comfortable, if not a more efficient way of conquering evil? If nothing else, why can't we enjoy the full fruits of Christ's resurrection now as we live the journey?

These questions might sound irreverent, but they probably have been asked in one form or another throughout the history of Christianity. The desire to have God eradicate human pain instead of just redeeming it began early in the experience of Christian belief. Soon after the resurrection, as the winds of Pentecost were still blowing through the early communities, an illusion threatened the early Christians: death is no more, many of them proclaimed; the Lord will come soon to raise us up; suffering is ended. The temptation to see life and the human condition as co-opted by the victory of Jesus was the source of painful disillusionment for many early Christians.

Slowly, through the preaching of Paul and the other prophets and apostles, the deeper truth began to dawn. The resurrection does not abolish the instructions of Jesus in the gospel; it confirms them. The message of the Sermon on the Mount and the beatitudes, Jesus' insistence on the daily cross (Lk 9:23), the teaching on the cost of discipleship—all these began to take on new personal meaning for the early communities of faith. If the master, "in order to enter into his glory" (Lk 24:26), has known tribulations and persecutions, the disciples must learn to follow the same way. The early Christians came to the conclusion slowly and painfully that the messianic era, which had already begun in Jesus, would nevertheless be a time of suffering and trial for them also.

Suffering with Christ: The Spirituality of Paul

The paschal mystery is not only the belief in Christ's redemptive journey through suffering and death. That same journey is being lived out now in our lives through faith. "It is no longer I who live," Paul tells his fellow Christians, "but Christ who lives in me" (Gal 2:20). The letters of Paul speak often of our solidarity with the risen Jesus: we suffer with Christ in order to be glorified with

him (Rm 8:17); we carry in our bodies the death of Jesus in
order that the new life of Jesus may also be manifest in our
bodies (II Cor 4:10); we embrace our weaknesses as a manifestation of the Lord's power (II Cor 11).

The divine response to the mystery of evil and suffering
is not a "solution" in the usual sense of the word. Instead
of taking suffering away, God simply comes to share it
with us. God's answer to our pain is the presence of Jesus.
Similarly, the Christian response to the same enigma is not
an "answer" in any logical sense, but a *way*—the commitment to unite our lives and suffering to the Lord and to
one another.

No one in the early Christian community better articulates this theology of union with Christ through suffering
than does the apostle Paul. His spirituality of suffering
does not arise from a theoretical framework but from his
experience as a disciple and a missionary. In common with
other prophetic figures in the Hebrew tradition, Paul
speaks of suffering within the context of his vocation to
proclaim the Word of God. In some ways Paul's temperament and struggle are not unlike those of Jeremiah. The
rabbi from Tarsus wrestles not only with the physical and
emotional hardships of his ministry, but also with his inner
contradictions and a persistent "thorn" in his flesh.

In light of his experience, it is understandable that Paul
would echo his Jewish forebears who saw suffering as
God's way of "educating" those chosen for service. Paul
understands his sufferings as God's way of leading him
away from unreality toward authentic life in Christ. Thus
in his letter to the Romans Paul says: "These sufferings
bring patience, as we know, and patience brings per-

serverance and perseverance brings hope, and this hope is not deceptive, because the love of God has been poured into our hearts by the Holy Spirit which has been given to us'' (Rm 5:3-5).

In any other setting these words might have a ring of Stoicism about them. But Paul is not a Stoic. He is not offering us a Christian version of ''grin and bear it;'' rather he is trying to describe the ineffable mystery of living daily in union with Christ. It is in this context that Paul embraces the times of personal rejection and disillusionment in his ministry. He comes to the point in his later writings in which he can actually ''rejoice'' in his sufferings (cf. II Cor 11-12). In one sense this is the supreme Christian irony: to rejoice, even to boast in those dimensions of human life which in any other setting could only be construed as failure and defeat.

Unfortunately, this is an irony which can easily be misconstrued, as the history of Christian spirituality indicates. Throughout the centuries there have been Christians who appear to believe that ''if it doesn't hurt, it isn't holy.'' By their attitudes and gloomy manner of living they imply that pain has some mystic value in itself apart from the mystery of redemption. This is clearly not Paul's intent. He can boast and rejoice in his failings and weakness only because they are joined to the redemptive journey of the risen Christ. To the Stoic or the non-believer his words would be as much of an absurdity as the cross itself.

The redemptive vision of suffering which Paul lived and preached can only be grasped within the eschatological or forward-looking hope which sustained his life and ministry. The energy of this vision is perhaps nowhere more powerfully stated than in these words which he wrote to the Philippians: "All I want is to know Christ and the power of his resurrection and to share his sufferings by reproducing the pattern of his death. That is the way I can hope to take my place in the resurrection of the dead. Not that I have become perfect yet: I have not yet won, but I am still running, trying to capture the prize for which Christ Jesus captured me. I can assure you my brothers I am far from thinking that I have already won. All I can say is that I forget the past and I strain ahead for what is still to come. I am racing for the finish, for the prize to which God calls us upwards to receive in Christ Jesus" (Philippians 3:10-14).

Questions for Reflection/Discussion

1. In what sense do you think that Jesus is or is not the "answer" to suffering and evil?

2. Discuss the various responses which Jesus makes to people who are in pain. What do these responses tell you about Jesus and his message? What response do they evoke in you?

3. Imagine that you have been asked to give a brief presentation to a small group on the "exorcism miracles" in the gospels. How would you approach the topic? What is the meaning of Jesus' "casting out" demons? What significance do these gospel accounts have for you?

4. The theologian Edward Schillebeeckx speaks of "the dangerous and subversive memory of Jesus of Nazareth."

What did Jesus say and do that made him so "dangerous and subversive"? In your opinion, why was Jesus put to death? What does his death reveal about the reality of evil?

5. What is central to Paul's spirituality of redemptive suffering? Is his approach meaningful to you? Why or why not?

Further Reading

Boff, Leonardo, *Jesus Christ Liberator* (Maryknoll, NY: Orbis Books, 1978).

Harrington, Wilfrid, O. P., *Mark,* Vol. 4 in the *New Testament Message* (Wilmington, Del: Michael Glazier, 1979).

Nolan, Albert, *Jesus Before Christianity* (Maryknoll, NY: Orbis Books, 1978).

Chapter 4

FAITH SEEKING UNDERSTANDING
Theology and the Mystery of Evil

THE collection of writings which we know as the Bible emerged slowly during several centuries of religious experience. They represent the collective memory of the chosen people as they encountered God and the dilemmas of human life. Inspired by the Spirit and rooted in human life, these writings provide us with a vivid description of the ways in which suffering and evil were confronted generation after generation. They speak of God's loving providence even in the face of what appears to be the oppression of the innocent and the outward success of evil. The scriptures also propose various responses to suffering —responses which find their culmination in the life, death, and resurrection of Jesus of Nazareth.

The gospels and the other New Testament writings, like the Hebrew scriptures, are already distinctive theologies of salvation. Some emphasize one aspect of redemptive suffering; others focus on another. Through it all an underlying truth emerges: the Word of God comes to us through the experience of the human person with all of its diversity and distinctiveness. The variety of responses to the problem of evil in the Hebrew scriptures is due, in part, to the influence of the other cultures and religions which surrounded Israel over the centuries. The Canaanites, the Egyptians, the Babylonians, and others all had some role in the questions and issues which the Jewish people pondered over the centuries. The bible is in some fashion a synthesis of these various influences, guided of course by the Holy Spirit and divine inspiration.

From the perspective of Catholic tradition, the definitive experience of God's revelation is said to have ended with the death of the last apostle. But this did not bring to a conclusion humanity's endeavor to probe the meaning of life's enigmas. The Word of God provides a pattern with which we can respond to the reality of suffering and evil, but it does not end the discussion. The questions remain, and so do the attempts to find new intellectual and theological insights. We will now explore the main lines of this theological tradition as it developed in the West.

Augustine: The Classic Theological Response of the West

As the Roman Empire began to decline, Christianity produced a thinker whose theological reflections would have an impact for centuries to come. His name was Aurelius Augustinus (354-430), better known in history as St. Augustine. Although he lived a somewhat fragmented life in his early years, there was a quality of restlessness, a hunger of the heart that drove Augustine onward. He was at heart a seeker of truth. His questioning mind led him through a variety of philosophical world-views until the preaching of Ambrose, the prayers of his mother Monica, and his hunger for God led him to conversion and a new life as a Christian.

At the age of forty-three, Augustine, now bishop of Hippo Regius and a respected Christian leader in North Africa, began to write his autobiography. The *Confessions* of St. Augustine is the story of his search for truth and his personal struggle with evil. His story has the capability of touching almost everyone's imagination in some way. In the early stages of his life's journey Augustine was a proud and cosmopolitan student. He frequented the circus and the theatre, he consulted astrologers and magicians, he struggled with his family and its values, he studied philosophy with a passion, and through it all he kept thirsting for the truth of his life.

At one point in his quest for truth Augustine embraced one of the most popular and powerful religious movements of the age. The Manichees were founded in the third century by the Persian prophet Mani, who believed that he had been given a direct revelation of the nature of God and the universe. So strongly did his teaching appeal to his contemporaries in the Roman empire and beyond, so lasting was its influence, that by the eighth century it had a hold as far east as China. Manicheanism was an appealing synthesis of various Gnostic belief systems, which offered a clear, dualistic explanation for the problem of evil. According to Mani, reality is a struggle between two equal and opposing powers: the Good, embodied in spirit and light; and the Evil, manifested in matter and darkness.

For eleven years Augustine followed the Manichean explanation of reality. He had long been searching for intellectual clarity and insight into his inner contradictions. The Manichees appealed to some deep tension within him, a feeling of being at war with himself. In short, they gave words to what Augustine himself had felt about his body and soul, "that they have been enemies since the creation of the worlds" (*Manichean Psalm Book* ccxlviii). The neoplatonist philosophers had already told him this truth as it applied to the self, but the Manichees went further and projected the picture on the wide screen of the cosmos. In effect, Mani's teachings relieved Augustine of the personal responsibility for his soul's health, and allowed him to cast his burden onto the universe. When he was young, Augustine notes wryly, he was much more willing to believe that the universe was out of joint than that there was something wrong with himself (cf. *Confessions* VII, iii, 4).

After a time Augustine discovered that the mystery of life could not be contained in the simplistic perspective of Mani. His mind and soul cried out for something more substantial and expansive, and in the end he rejected Manicheanism in favor of belief in one God who is all good and the sole source of all reality. After his conversion to Christianity in the early fifth century Augustine combined concepts of Greek philosophy (especially those of Plato) with the vision of the gospel to combat the Manichean explanation of the problem of evil. One of the distinctive characteristics of his theology of evil is that he developed it as an answer to his former belief system.

Augustine tells the story of his life as a Manichean, his wrestling with the problem of evil, and the solution he finally arrived at in his *Confessions,* Books 4-7. The questions he faced were not abstract or theoretical; they arose from his former way of thinking. The dualistic explanation for the problem of evil was simple and, in its own way, satisfying. Christians, like their Hebrew ancestors in faith, had to face the difficult questions which flow from a belief in one God. If the creator of the world is good, then what is evil and whence does it come? This is the central issue which Augustine addresses in his writings and which we summarize here.

1) *Evil as the Absence of Good.* During his years as a Manichean, Augustine had resolved the problem of evil by maintaining that matter is evil and not the creation of a loving and good God. Salvation takes place when the soul escapes from the kingdom of darkness (the body) into the kingdom of light (the spirit). With his conversion to Christianity, Augustine rejected this teaching. At the same time he was left with an enigma. He knew from his experience that evil is a reality and not just an illusion. He recognized, in other words, that he could not explain evil by explaining it away. His solution was to maintain that evil is a negativity in being, an absence of a positive good that should be present. In short, evil is a privation of being.

According to Augustine, everything that is, to the extent that it is something positive, is good. It becomes evil only when it ceases to be what it should be. For example, physical blindness in a human being is an evil, since humans are created in such a fashion as to be able to see with their eyes. Likewise, the fact that a tree or a rock cannot see is not considered to be evil, since on the hierarchical ladder of being they are not created in such a fashion that vision is part of their metaphysical makeup. Evil is only present where there is an actual lack of goodness or reality in a situation where it ought to be present.

2) *Free Will as the Source of Moral Evil or Sin.* One of the basic assumptions in Augustine's theology is that God created the world in his image and likeness—that is, in the image of his goodness. But if God is good and created the world and its creatures as an expression of his goodness, then where does evil come from? The answer is the human

capacity for free will and personal responsibility. According to Augustine, God created woman and man to be free creatures. He gave them the dignity of freedom so their response would not be that of a slave or a mechanical robot, but the freely willed response of love. Thus God's love created a situation of risk, a situation in which it is possible for human beings to fail in the very act which otherwise enables them to love freely and achieve maturity.

In the history of salvation, human rebellion turned the possibility of evil into a reality. Striving to be independent from God, human beings have chosen to center their freedom on their own autonomy instead of in relationship to God. This act of rebellion is sin, and the essence of sin is a disordered relationship of free will toward God.

3) *Suffering as the Result of Sin.* The misuse of freedom in human selfishness is a choice which alienated woman and man from God. Sin had repercussions, most of which were devastating for human happiness. In the wake of this primal disorder, according to Augustine, all the other relationships in creation also went awry. Human beings found themselves out of joint with creation, with each other, and even with their own deepest selves. Like a destructive tidal wave, sin flowed over into a variety of painful consequences. Because of sin there is sorrow, the burden of work, disease, weakness, fragility, and widespread suffering in the world.

St. Augustine makes a careful distinction regarding the consequences of human sinfulness. He points out that we do not necessarily suffer the results of our own personal sins. We suffer because we are born into a world which is broken and fragmented by the sins of the past. We enter a sinful situation. Our suffering flows from this condition of brokenness as well as the ways in which we further this condition by our own personal sins. From Augustine's point of view, it is not unjust that we suffer from the consequences of sin, since we are all somehow implicated in the original fall.

4) *God's Love Overcomes Sin and Suffering.* Having explored the nature and consequences of evil, Augustine moves on to describe the reasons for our hope. He speaks of God's eternal providence in overcoming our brokenness through redemptive love. Evil would never have been permitted to enter creation through human freedom if God were not able to draw from it an even greater good. Just as love made sin possible by creating women and men as free creatures, so an even greater love redeems this brokenness and turns tragedy into healing. God's infinite wisdom transforms rebellion into redemption.

For Augustine the history of salvation is a revelation of divine mercy and justice. It is a manifestation of mercy because God freely offers grace and forgiveness to all human beings, even those who continue to persist in sin and selfishness. It is likewise a sign of divine justice because God condemns to hell those who will not accept the gift of unconditional love. In the suffering of Jesus human pain and tragedy are redeemed and given meaning. Christians find in their daily crosses an opportunity to share in the sufferings and redemptive work of Christ. Thus Augustine echoes the earlier Hebrew themes which describe suffering as a way of being tested in virtue, growing in wisdom, and an opportunity for deeper union with God by uniting oneself to the sufferings of the Lord.

Most Catholics who grew up before the Second Vatican Council would be familiar with Augustine's theology from studying the catechism or listening to sermons at a parish mission. Augustine's personal and theoretical reflections on suffering and evil became the classic church teaching of Western Christianity and continue to have a major influence today.

Aquinas: The Classic Theory Confirmed

The influential doctor of the church who enabled Augustine's view to prevail in Western Christianity was Thomas Aquinas (1225-1274). Except for a few modifications traceable mainly to Aristotle, the main elements of Augustine's thought are embodied in the theology of Aquinas. St. Thomas inherited the metaphysical model of act and potency from Aristotle as a way of understanding the structure of reality. "Every nature," Aquinas writes, "is either act or potency or a composite of the two. Whatever is act, is a perfection and is good in its very concept. And what is in potency has a natural appetite for the reception of act; but what all beings desire is good" (*Sum. Theol.* I, Quest. 48, Art. 3).

Implicit in Aquinas' position is the conviction that every nature or being, whether fully realized or in potential toward realization, is basically good. This reiterates from a slightly different perspective what Augustine had written eight centuries earlier: evil is simply the absence of good, the privation of perfect being. Nothing can be evil in itself.

Evil can exist only in something good as its subject, since as a lack of being or a privation, it needs a substratum or foundation which is a being and hence good.

This is not the same as saying that evil is merely a negation of being. Rather, as Jacques Maritain points out in his commentary on Aquinas, it is a *privation*—the lack of a good that should be in a thing or creature. In short, evil can only exist in the good, and it can only work through the good. It wounds and malforms the good and causes a basic disorder in creation with resulting suffering and pain for human beings and the rest of God's creatures.

Obviously there were other church writers and theologians besides Augustine and Thomas who addressed the problem of suffering and evil. St. Basil the Great (c.330-379), one of the most formative figures in Eastern monasticism, developed a theory of evil which synthesized the Christian scriptures with the neoplatonic ideas of Plotinus. Even before Augustine, Basil had elaborated an understanding of evil as the deprivation of good. He dedicated an entire work to the topic, *God Is Not The Author of Evil.* In the same vein, Origen and John Chrysostom preached and wrote about the universal providence of God even in the face of human suffering. Clement, Cyril, Ambrose, and others developed the theme of Jesus as suffering servant and death as the gateway to life.

But the classic statement of church doctrine was formulated in an enduring way by Augustine and given fresh perspective by Aquinas. For the most part, it is this explanation of evil and suffering which the church incorporated into its official teaching on the subject.

We can summarize the main features of this teaching as follows:

1) There is one God, almighty and all-good, who is the one source of all of creation.

2) Creation is itself an image of its maker and therefore good, though limited because it is a creature.

3) Human beings were created in the divine image in a preternatural state of happiness and friendship with God.

4) Evil and suffering do not come from God, but are the result of the sin of angels (demons) and humans who rebelled against God.

5) As a result of this fall from grace, human nature is "wounded" or "blinded." Because of "original sin" we are born into a broken world of suffering and death. We stand in desperate need of salvation from God.

6) It is in God's loving plan and within the realm of divine power to overcome the dominion of the "evil one" and to redeem the sufferings of creation.

7) God overcomes evil and makes suffering redemptive in the life, death, and resurrection of Jesus, the Son of God and the suffering Servant.

8) Christians share in the redemptive power of Christ through baptism and by living out the paschal mystery

daily. Through solidarity with the risen Lord their sufferings and those of their brothers and sisters can be transformed into life-giving sacrifice.

Irenaeus: An Alternate Approach

Before we address the issue of recent church teaching on the topic of suffering and evil, it is important to examine an early alternative to the traditional Augustinian view, one which has been rediscovered and re-emphasized as a source for several present-day theologies of evil.

This vision was first formulated by Irenaeus (c. 120-200), a native of Asia Minor, who as a missionary in Gaul became the bishop of present-day Lyons in 177. There are significant areas of agreement between Irenaeus and Augustine. Both of them, for instance, reject a dualistic solution and look to God as the ultimate source of all reality. However, Irenaeus has an understanding of creation and the role of human beings which gives his theology a developmental rather than a static context.

In Augustine's perspective human beings were created perfect but fell from grace because of a free and culpable act of rebellion against God. This disobedience disrupted the divine plan and introduced evil into the world. All human beings inherit Adam's guilt, and their sufferings are divine punishment for sin. In contrast to this point of view, Irenaeus maintains that God did not create humans in a primitive state of perfection, but in a childlike condition of openness to growth. Women and men were created in an early stage of developmental awareness with the capacity and the call to grow toward moral and human wholeness. Within this evolutionary perspective Irenaeus works out what might be described as an early "theology of development." Although human beings are created in the "image" of God, they still have to grow through free choice and struggle into the "likeness" of God. In this view the fall of Adam is understood as an occurrence in the "childhood of the species," a lapse that can be attributed to our early immaturity. This changes the meaning of sin as it relates to the reality of suffering and evil in the world. Sin is not understood as a disaster which badly wounded the human condition; rather it is viewed as a painful but challenging call to grow toward authentic human wholeness. Irenaeus was developing what today might be described as a "teleological" context for understanding sin and evil. The Greek word *telos* refers to the goal or destiny which is intrinsic to the very essence of a creature—the most profound tendency of its being. A teleological perspective on sin attempts to understand it in the broader unfolding of the history of salvation. It emphasizes that even in the human encounter with brokenness the divine purpose is at work slowly and patiently shaping human experience toward its ultimate goal of union with God.

Irenaeus believed that the encounter with good and evil is part of the growing process of human consciousness. Only by experiencing the tension between choices and options can we learn to cherish that which leads us to growth and to reject those experiences which lead us into isolation and brokenness. In his approach sin does not ruin or corrupt the human condition; it delays it, challenges it, and clarifies the trajectory which leads toward wholeness and union with the divine. Every human person is called to enter life as an "image" of the divine and to grow, with the help of grace, toward becoming the "likeness" of God.

This journey toward moral and personal maturity is interrupted and delayed by "the Fall," but it is renewed by the incarnation of God in Jesus and carried forward by the activity of the Holy Spirit.

Until recently the Irenaean perspective on sin and suffering was at best "a minority report" in Western theology. The Augustinian solution to the problem of evil has held the dominant position in ordinary Catholic teaching up until the last three or four decades. All the same, like a persistent thread in the tapestry of Christian theology, this minority report continued to be studied and discussed. The teleological understanding of human life was shared by Clement of Alexandria and, to some extent, by Gregory of Nazianzus. It has also been part of Eastern Orthodox theology from the second century to the present, and frequently finds its way into our liturgy. The theme of God's grace transforming evil toward redemptive growth is strikingly expressed in the ancient Latin of the "Exsultet" which is sung at the Easter Vigil: *"O felix culpa quae talem ac tantum meruit habere redemptorem"*—"O fortunate fault which merited so great a redeemer."

Questions for Reflection/Discussion

1. How would you describe the main stages in Augustine's inner journey which led to his theology of suffering and evil? What role did Manicheanism play in that journey? Is there anything about the approach of Mani that attracts you?

2. Evaluate Augustine's explanation of the origin and reality of evil. What aspects of his theology are most ap-

pealing to you? What elements do you find unclear or un-satisfying?

3. How do you evaluate the perspective of Irenaeus regarding the problem of evil? Compare and contrast his position with Augustine's. What are the strengths and weaknesses of each?

4. From your point of view, why do you think Augustine's theology became the classic expression of the church's teaching in the Middle Ages rather than that of Irenaeus?

Further Reading

Aquinas, St. Thomas, *Selected Writings,* trans. and notes by Robert P. Goodwin (Indianapolis: Bobbs-Merrill, 1965).

Bourke, Vernon J., ed., *The Essential Augustine* (New York: New American Library, 1964).

Maritain, Jacques, *St. Thomas and the Problem of Evil* (Milwaukee: Marquette University Press, 1942).

Quasten, Johannes, *Patrology,* Two Volumes (West-minster, Md: Newman Press, 1962).

Chapter 5

THE NEW MOMENT
Recent Church Teaching On Suffering And Evil

A Change of Context

WHATEVER the differences which exist among patristic writers regarding specific theological issues, they nevertheless share a common world-view. What is distinctive about their way of thinking? In what sense is the context of the church fathers different from the modern encounter with evil and suffering?

For the most part, it is a modern issue to see a tension between the wisdom of God and the suffering of the innocent. Neither the scriptures nor the early writers who formulated the classic Catholic theology of evil have a problem reconciling the pain of this world with the providence of God. In the tradition of Israel evil did not pose a direct problem in respect to divine wisdom, which "reaches from end to end mightily, and orders all things sweetly" (Wis 8:1).

Even in the book of Job, it is clear that the justice of God is never brought into question. The issue for the author of Job is to establish that a suffering person can also be just, instead of the usual assumption that where there is suffering there is automatically sinfulness. Job's suffering is portrayed as an exemplary test of virtue. Throughout his ordeal he continues to be confident that God recognizes his integrity and judges him accordingly (cf Job 31:6). The climax of Job's story is the encounter with

God in which he realizes that the human mind and heart cannot comprehend the mystery of divine governance. We must simply trust that God's ways are ultimately providential.

This assumption in favor of God's goodness and care is expressed in the writings of Christian theologians from Augustine to Gregory the Great. Suffering and pain, no matter how intense they might be, are understood as somehow within the providence of a loving God. Whatever the calamities or however widespread their destruction, they are not seen as a reason for questioning the merciful designs of the Creator.

This is not to say that the early church writers are blind to the reality or the intensity of evil. They are as sensitive to the mystery of suffering as any group of religious thinkers ever were. The difference in perspective is related to the manner in which they view the reality of suffering. No matter how widespread the pain or catastrophe, they see it as somehow under the power of God. Human pain is real; the presence of satanic forces is real; but this is not a reason to doubt God's providence. In the words of Julian of Norwich, "the power of the fiend is locked in God's hand."

This confidence in God's providence has been severely shaken in modern times. With the gradual process of secularization the religious experience of awe has receded or become more privatized. Even more threatening to humankind's trust in God has been the emergence of technologies of war and the capacity for global destruction. The 20th century may well be remembered as an era of unparalleled destruction and violence. In the face of the Holocaust and Hiroshima the belief in God's loving design for the world is radically called into question. The religious thinkers of our time speak more often of the "death of God" or the "eclipse of God" than of a loving providence at work in history. However much the creator and sustainer of life may love and redeem the universe, there is still the awesome reality of human freedom with its capacity to continue the creative process or to choose self-destruction.

In what way has the theological issue of suffering and evil changed? It is not that the traditional theory as articulated by Augustine and other early church writers is incorrect or theologically mistaken. Rather, it is the horizon of human experience which has been transformed and which cries out for a different response. The present generation of humanity, which Alvin Toffler has called "the 800th lifetime," has endured the devastation of the Second World War. We know about Nagasaki and Hiroshima. We have experienced the Nazi gas ovens, Korea, Vietnam, African famines, cancer, AIDS, Chernobyl, and Three Mile Island. In our imaginations, if not in our lives, we carry images of people who died through obliteration bombing or political mass murders. We have daily news reports regarding the exploitation of people through apartheid or other oppressive forms of government. We have learned to live with the daily possibility of global nuclear war.

In the face of such terrifying forms of evil the classical solutions to the mystery of suffering leave us cold and untouched. Instinctively we know that it is no longer sufficient to speak of evil as a privation. It is not enough to say "avoid evil" when we are confronted daily with political repression in Africa, Latin America, and Eastern Europe. The spiraling arms race and the prospect of "Star Wars" move us into a radically different setting of human reflection. In short, we have arrived at a new time in human-kind's encounter with the mystery of darkness.

The New Moment

In their pastoral letter *The Challenge of Peace* (1983), the United States bishops speak of a "new moment" in human history. In the context of their statement, the bishops use this phrase to describe the destructive capacity of weapons today. From time immemorial human beings have engaged in warfare, but never before have they had the capacity of creating what some scientists have described as a "nuclear winter."

But the bishops also see a hopeful side to this "new moment." It is possible, they tell us, to turn the tide of history toward life and the beginnings of true peace on our planet. In other words, the "new moment" is a reality which goes beyond the technologies of war or even the strategies of peace. The new moment is a way of describing a significant turning point in the history of humankind's relationship to God and the world. Philosophers of culture speak of entering the post-industrial, post-modern era. Theologians describe a "paradigm shift" in human self-understanding or a new "axial period" in human awareness. We are obviously groping for ways to express something which is not yet fully clear to us.

What is the deeper meaning of the "new moment"? What brought about this new stage in human history? What implications does it have for a theology of suffering and evil? We will address these questions before examining their impact on the church's current teaching.

1) *The Technological Revolution.* It took humankind more than two million years to move from the use of blunt instruments to developing sharp tools and weapons. It has taken less than seventy years in this century for human beings to go from the sands of Kitty Hawk to the craters of the moon. The scientific changes which have occurred in this age are so sweeping that we cannot begin to comprehend their impact or their implications. From computers to communication satellites, from organ transplants to genetics, from radio astronomy to Trident submarines, the tide of technological transformation continues to expand.

What we cannot so easily measure is the effect which this revolution is having on human life and values. Tools are, in some fundamental way, an extension of the human body. They enable us to shape and use the resources of creation in ways that transcend our physical strength or dexterity. In a similar way computers also project the human brain beyond itself in a new way of interacting with the world and its resources. As we gain greater capacity to control the energy of the earth, a fundamental question is raised: are we part of creation or somehow above it? Can we continue to develop our technology without taking into account the fundamental issues of ecology and our place as a creature among other creatures?

More than forty years ago Romano Guardini wrote that the fundamental moral issue for the rest of this century will be the question of how we will use scientific power. Technology has become a tool both of control and of decision. It is no longer just a question of what we *can* do with our scientific instruments; it is an issue of what we *ought* to do with them. We have brought ourselves to the edge of human freedom and responsibility. In our time the greatest evils are not those which might arise from natural disasters, but those which human beings are now capable of bringing upon themselves.

2) *Global Awareness*. In addition to influencing our understanding of scientific responsibility, the technological advances of the last fifty years have had another important effect on human experience. They have transformed the world into a global village. The enduring symbol of this change in awareness is the photograph of an earthrise which was transmitted to us from a manned spacecraft as it emerged from the dark side of the moon. It was literally the first time we had seen our planet from that vantage point. What we viewed was not a vast expanse of land and water masses with distinct boundaries for national sovereignty, but a small blue planet, fragile and limited against the immensity of space. The earth appeared on the horizon of the universe like a glistening beacon of life, a cosmic spacecraft with its own life-support system and a limited amount of resources. This striking photo told us what statistics and other data cannot tell us, namely, that we are living in a radically interdependent world. The future of the human race and the survival of the planet are inextricably linked to each other.

The second symbol of our interdependence arises from the widening network of telecommunications which surrounds the globe. Today there is the possibility of nearly instantaneous contact and information sharing with the rest of the human community. The effect of this communications network is still beyond our comprehension. In the words of the late Lyndon B. Johnson, "the world has become a neighborhood before it has become a brotherhood." This statement may be framed in sexist language, but it conveys a stark truth nonetheless. Our technology has not only made our world more fragile, it has also reduced its proportions. Whether or not nations are willing to recognize it, a smaller world is also a more interdependent world. The famine in Africa, the network of international terrorism, the political oppression in Latin America, the arms race between the U.S. and the U.S.S.R.—all of these realities have an impact on other segments of the global village. They are brought into our living rooms and offices with stereo sound and in living color. It is no longer practical for us to pretend that we can live in isolation from the rest of the international community. In the most fundamental sense the age of nation-states is over.

Whether our thinking will catch up with these historical realities is another question. The economist Kenneth Boulding contends that if the human race is to survive, "it will have to change its ways of thinking more in the next 25 years than it has in the last 25,000."

3) *The Emergence of Historical Consciousness.* The third dimension of "the new moment" in which the human race finds itself is a growing awareness that we have history "in our hands." The future is no longer something that will simply happen to us; it is a reality that we are in some way responsible for shaping. In earlier times the world and the human role in it were viewed in more static terms. Some aspects of our religious heritage even tended to downplay the value and meaning of this world and its history. Our

goal, this perspective reminded us, is to leave the earth behind for heaven. Our task is to save our souls, not to build the earth. One of the reasons why the church fathers rarely asked why God permits the suffering of the innocent is that, in their view, the Christian faith rests on the belief in a future life. Their focus was for the most part other-worldly. They viewed human life as a pilgrimage through a vale of tears toward the true promised land.

Where did this other-worldly perspective find its roots? There is evidence in the New Testament writings that the early Christian community expected the *eschaton,* or the end of the world, to take place soon. Paul frequently exhorted his fellow believers to be prepared for the Lord's return. His response to suffering takes place within this conviction that the world is rapidly passing away: "I reckon that the sufferings of this time are not worthy to be compared with the glory that is to come which shall be revealed in us" (Rm 8:18).

Even after it became clear that the *eschaton* was probably not going to take place tomorrow or in the next year, most of the early church fathers nonetheless kept an other-worldly focus. History was understood as a static realm, a kind of waiting room, in which human life is tested by pain and graced by love, and then moves forward to the eternal life of heaven. In the words of John Keats, our earthly life is a "vale of soul-making," with high priority placed on preparation for the next life. In this view of history there is little emphasis on the call to care for the earth or to build the reign of God. History is in God's hands; we are merely wayfarers who endure its pain as we pursue our eternal salvation.

In the last two centuries this understanding of history has begun to undergo a radical transformation. Technology and our emerging global awareness have contributed to a growing sense of responsibility for creation and history. History can no longer be understood merely as those experiences and events which happen *to* us. In comparison to the 20 billion year history of creation, human beings are fragile latecomers. At the same time, because human life represents evolution becoming conscious of itself, we have inherited both the gift and the responsibility of continuing the cosmic journey toward expanded life.

In short, the revolution in technology and science has in turn created the need for a transformed view of history. This does not lessen the reality of evil. If anything, its presence is all the more disturbing since the possibilities of even greater destruction and pain lie within the power of human beings. The difference lies in the manner in which we now confront the human dilemma. At a time of emerging historical consciousness, evil is no longer viewed as mystery we endure but as a reality which we are called to fight against and alleviate.

The New Moment and Recent Church Teaching

When he convened the Second Vatican Council, Pope John XXIII challenged the church to "read the signs of the times," a phrase which is taken from the Hebrew prophets and their role as sentinels for God's people. To read the signs of the times is to discern the meaning of one's era. It involves far more than familiarizing oneself with the current trends or fashionable ideas of the day. The deeper prophetic task is to listen to the hungers of the human heart and the mysterious ways in which God's reign is breaking into life in any age. Reading the signs of the times also implies that the church, as the extension of God's incarnation in Jesus, enters into and shapes the energies of life according to the contours of the gospel.

We are now closer in time to the beginning of the third millennium of Christianity than we are to the Second Vatican Council. From the vantage point of time, we are beginning to understand some things that may not have been as clear earlier. It is more obvious now, for instance, that Vatican II did not *cause* the profound change which has swept through the church; it only gave voice and shape to energies which were already at work in our world and in the Christian community. At the deepest level the church had already begun to enter the "new moment." It initiated this response long before the bishops of the world gathered at St. Peter's Basilica in the fall of 1962.

Leo XIII: The Emergence of a New Perspective

What are some of the indicators that the church's teaching was beginning to develop in new directions? The first signs of a change in the church's stance toward the problem of evil can be seen as early as Leo XIII's *Rerum Novarum* (On The Condition of the Laborer) in 1891. Prior to this time, the church tended to maintain a suspicious attitude toward the earth and human history. It had inherited an other-worldly spirituality from many of the church fathers—an attitude which was, with few exceptions, affirmed by the medieval scholastics and strengthened by the church's defensive posture during the Counter-Reformation. Even as late as Pius IX the church found itself standing apart from the intellectual, scientific, and technological currents of the age, condemning a rather vague enemy described simply as "modernism."

During most of this period the church relied on the formulation of the problem of evil which it had inherited from Augustine and the medieval theologians. It portrayed the world as the battleground between light and darkness, where individual members of the "Church Militant" worked out their eternal salvation by accepting life's pain and uniting themselves to the redemptive work of Christ.

Prior to 1891 the magisterium had not articulated a clear commitment on the church's part to work for justice in the world or to change the structures which reinforce human oppression. In *Rerum Novarum,* Leo XIII enunciated an initial role for the church in supporting efforts for just wages and the right of working people to organize. This was the beginning of an important development in the church's stance toward injustice and evil in the world. But it was only a beginning. In the late 19th century the church's focus was on the working class of Europe, with the Vatican understanding its role primarily as teacher. During the 20th century both the focus and role have changed considerably. The church has begun to perceive itself less in the paternalistic manner of a teacher and more as a compassionate and prophetic presence on behalf of the poor and the oppressed throughout the world.

Toward a Global Response to Suffering and Evil

As early as Pius XII and his encyclical *Mystici Corporis* (1943), the church began widening its perspective beyond the working class of Europe to include the universality of all people. With the documents of Vatican II and the writings of recent popes the vision of church concern became truly global. John XXIII and Paul VI spoke with increasing urgency regarding the needs of the whole world, especially developing countries, minorities, refugees, women, youth, and any group of people who faced the conditions of injustice. The mission of the church was seen to be more active in its struggle against evil and the oppression which flows from sinful structures.

The call of the church to oppose injustice reached its climax in the teachings of the Second Vatican Council, especially in the Pastoral Constitution on the Church in the Modern World (*Gaudium et Spes*). This document begins with these memorable words: "The joy and hope, the grief and anguish of the people of our age, especially of those who are poor or afflicted in any way, are the joy and hope, the grief and anguish of the followers of Christ as well." This world-involving attitude of Christian mission is further intensified in the document *Justice In The World,* issued by the 1971 Synod of Bishops. In the tradition of the ancient prophets, the bishops declare that "action on behalf of justice and participation in the transformation of the world fully appear to us as a constitutive dimension of the preaching of the gospel, or in other words of the church's mission for the redemption of the human race and its liberation from every oppressive situation."

This does not mean that the church has set aside its emphasis on transcendence or the importance of the next world. Contemporary church teaching still maintains the creative tension between the here and the hereafter, but it is responding to the mandate of making peace and building justice with a greater sense of urgency than ever before in its history. We would probably search in vain for a statement in the early Christian writers which would parallel this vision of *Gaudium et Spes:* "While rejecting atheism outright, the church sincerely professes that all people, believers and unbelievers alike, ought to work for the betterment of the world in which we live" (#21). The same is true of these words from *Lumen Gentium:* "The church encompasses with love all those who are afflicted with human weakness. Indeed she recognizes in the poor and suffering the likeness of her poor and suffering Founder. She does all she can to relieve their need and in them she strives to serve Christ" (#8).

There is an assumption in the church's contemporary social teaching that the global struggle against "the powers of darkness which has pervaded all of human history" (*Gaudium et Spes* #37) is now a personal and communal mandate for all Christians. Every believer has a prophetic call to oppose evil and alleviate suffering, instead of passively accepting it as a condition of human life. Obviously this refers primarily to our opposition to moral evil and its consequences in the world. There are still many forms of physical evil—natural disasters and other experiences of suffering—which we can neither avoid nor prevent. Even in these instances, however, the call to respond with compassion toward the victims is unequivocal.

The Vision of John Paul II

Any summary of current church teaching regarding suffering and evil would be incomplete without taking into account the contribution of Pope John Paul II. From the perspective of human and religious experience, Karol Wojtyla's life might well be considered a profile of the 20th century. His life spans the devastation of two world wars and their fearful aftermath. He grew up in a country which has repeatedly encountered the suffering of occupying armies and oppressive ideologies. He has witnessed the mystery of suffering in his native Poland while growing up and during his ministry as priest and bishop. More recently he has reached out to the poor of the world through his global travels as leader of the Roman Catholic Church. In addition, he has survived an assassin's bullet and journeyed through the darkness of pain in his own life.

Understandably, there is a deep sensitivity in John Paul II for the suffering of the world and a concern for the form and shape which evil has taken in our day. From Puebla to Calcutta his journeys have taken him to places where people have encountered the pain of poverty, starvation, and political oppression. It is remarkable to see how many of John Paul's public addresses are dedicated to the topic of suffering and its redemptive possibilities.

In addition to his many sermons and speeches on the topic, John Paul II has written several documents which touch upon the theme of suffering and the problem of evil, including parts of *Redemptor Hominis* (Redeemer of Humankind, 1979) and *Laborem Exercens* (On the Dignity of Human Labor, 1981). By far the most significant of his writings on the topic, however, is his apostolic letter *Salvifici Doloris* (On the Christian Meaning of Human Suffering), which he published in 1984 as part of the "Holy Year of the Redemption."

The doctrinal stance which the pope takes in *Salvifici*

Doloris might be characterized as "continuity in a context of change." As is the case in most of his writings, John Paul II is concerned in this document with re-emphasizing the traditional and perduring qualities of Catholic teaching, while at the same time taking into account the distinctive characteristics of human experience today. The result is a reflection on suffering which integrates the traditional perspective with the church's recent focus on Christian responsibility.

In the first part of the apostolic letter, John Paul reaffirms the classical Augustinian stance toward suffering while expanding and deepening its scriptural basis. He describes evil as a privation of good and suffering as a consequence of sin. At the same time he is careful to point out that "while it is true that suffering has a meaning as punishment when it is connected with a fault, it is not true that all suffering is a consequence of a fault and has the nature of a punishment" (#11). He also explores the "educational" value of suffering and emphasizes that in order for suffering to have Christian meaning it must always be seen as a call to deeper conversion.

If there is a reaffirmation of traditional Catholic teaching in this apostolic letter, there is also evidence that John Paul intends to develop further some aspects of recent church teaching. There is, for instance, a strong emphasis in this document on the responsibility of Christians to transform society by resisting evil and by reaching out to those who suffer. This developmental aspect of John Paul's vision arises from his theology of salvation, which he articulated in *Redemptor Hominis* and applies consistently here. He specifically describes salvation as "liberation from evil" (14).

Obviously Jesus is the model of one who liberates others from evil by taking suffering upon himself. Because "Christ suffers voluntarily and innocently" (#18), his pain becomes redemptive and liberating. John Paul also speaks of the ways in which Christians share in the redemptive sufferings of Christ. The pope outlines what he calls "The Gospel of Suffering" (#25). This gospel was first "written" by Jesus when he accepted his sufferings out of love for others. It continues to be written in the lives of Christians who unite their sufferings and their efforts on behalf of liberation with those of the risen Christ (#26).

The Gospel of Suffering continues to be written today, according to John Paul, whenever Christians enflesh the parable of the Good Samaritan in their lives. The suffering of other people is redemptive only if it evokes a response of compassion in us. "We are not allowed to 'pass by on the other side' indifferently; we must 'stop' beside the suffering one. Everyone who stops beside the suffering of another person, whatever form it may take, is a Good Samaritan" (#28). "Stopping at the side" of suffering people takes on the same active meaning today as it did for the Samaritan in Jesus' parable. To underline this call to action in the face of suffering, John Paul makes this remarkable statement: "The salvific meaning of suffering is in no way identified with an attitude of passivity . . . the gospel is the negation of passivity in the face of suffering" (#30).

Active solidarity on behalf of those who suffer is not limited to the level of personal compassion. John Paul speaks of Jesus' mission as a "messianic program" (#30), implying that the reign of God transforms structures and societal attitudes as well as healing individuals. The church, as the extension of the risen Christ in time and space, has the mission "to transform the whole of human civilization into a civilization of love" (#30).

Questions for Reflection/Discussion

1. Several theologians have suggested that technology is morally "neutral," i.e., neither good nor bad in itself. Do you see technological progress as a possible instrument to help overcome evil? How does it present the danger of even greater evil?

2. The United States bishops believe that we have arrived at a "new moment" in human history. How would you describe this new moment in your own words? What implications does this have for the Christian struggle against evil? For your own life and values?

3. How is the "new moment" reflected in recent church teaching? Try to give some examples from your reading of church documents since the Second Vatican Council. Do you feel comfortable in committing yourself to this new emphasis on action and personal responsibility?

4. Some contemporary Catholics feel that the church has become too involved in the political and social sphere. What is your opinion? Do you think the church can become committed to making peace and creating a just world without losing the "transcendent" dimension of faith? What pitfalls do you envision?

Further Reading

Flannery, Austin, O. P., ed., *Vatican II: The Conciliar and Post Conciliar Documents* (Northport, NY: Costello Publishing Co., 1975).

O'Brien, David, and Shannon, Thomas, eds., *Renewing The Earth: Catholic Documents on Peace, Justice, and Liberation* (Maryknoll, NY: Orbis Books, 1977).

Pope John Paul II, *Salvifici Doloris* (Boston: St. Paul Editions, 1984). Also from the same publisher: *Laborem Exercens, Dives in Misericordia,* and *Redemptor Hominis.*

United States Conference of Catholic Bishops, *The Challenge of Peace: God's Promise and Our Response,* A Pastoral Letter on Peace and War (Washington, DC: USCC Publications, 1983).

Chapter 6

SOUNDS OF SORROW, VOICES OF HOPE
Contemporary Approaches To Suffering And Evil

IN the 1930s the French Socialist Georges Sorel, who was a friend of Charles Peguy and whose books were read carefully by Mussolini and Lenin, told his students that the crucial work of philosophers, in the new age which they were about to enter, would "consist in recasting and penetrating more deeply into the problem of evil." Though Sorel is little remembered today, his prophecy regarding the problem of evil in this "new age" has certainly been realized. Philosophers and theologians of varying persuasions and backgrounds have brought their intellectual and reflective energies to bear on the topic. But it is no longer a case of intellectuals spinning out "theodicies" in the isolation of their classrooms or offices. The issue of suffering and evil has moved beyond the realm of the academy and scholarly journals to involve justice and peace committees, hospital ethics boards, environmental groups, and most of the concerned citizens who care about the future of this planet.

In this chapter we will explore this contemporary debate as it has affected the teaching and mission of the church and the attitudes and lives of individual believers. Not surprisingly, the spectrum of theological opinion is wide and varied. It ranges from the theoretical to the practical, from the prophetic to the apocalyptic. We shall examine eight different stances or movements which are continuing to influence our understanding of suffering and evil and the church's responsibility to articulate a coherent theological vision on this vital issue.

1. The Classical View Restated

In this century there have been several philosophers and theologians who have attempted to update and restate the classical Augustinian perspective on the nature of evil and suffering. These authors include such respected theologians as Martin D'Arcy, C. S. Lewis, and Charles Journet and philosophers such as Alvin Platinga and Stephen Davis. While they rely on the basic framework of Augustine's line of reasoning, these thinkers have also taken into account this century's heightened encounter with war, violence, and human suffering. They have emphasized that the reality of pain and darkness in our time is an intense and existentially real human experience, while at the same time insisting that evil has no essence or ontic ground of its own. Evil, they have maintained, is good that has been disordered and deranged by the misuse of free will and human creativity.

This restatement of the Augustinian argument bears all the characteristics of a traditional "theodicy" (a word derived from the Greek *theos* (God) and *dike* (justice), which has as its primary purpose to "justify" the existence of evil and suffering in a world created by an all powerful and all good God. Like its original counterpart, this "solution" to the problem of evil has some important theological advantages. It preserves the transcendent freedom of God and explains how divine grace can remain sovereign and undefeated even when it is resisted by the sinfulness of human beings. It stresses, as some of the other perspectives do not, the metaphysical chasm between being and non-being, between truth and error, between good as positive and evil as privative. This traditional position also maintains that the widespread suffering in this century is a consequence of human selfishness and blindness of heart.

But there are also some serious deficiencies in this classical approach to the problem of evil. No matter how practical its proponents attempt to make it, the argument remains in essence a metaphysical explanation whose origins are located as much in a Platonic and Aristotelian world-view as they are in the Hebrew and Christian scriptures. Despite the updating of language and examples, this approach tends to sound like an abstract argument for an existential mystery.

Whatever logical consistency the Augustinian theodicy might have, it is lacking in personal meaning for those who are in pain or facing the injustice of oppression. The actual experience of suffering is more likely to generate anger or despair than the serene conviction that it is privative and ultimately unreal. What consolation can the oppressed *campesino* or the tortured political prisoner find in the belief that evil is only a corruption of the good? Does it make the pain or the personal indignity any more bearable?

Critics of this position also point out another inconsistency. The Augustinian approach maintains that all suffering is in some way a consequence of sin. It is obvious to most of us that human selfishness has a great deal of adverse fallout, ranging from wars to poverty to environmental damage. On the other hand, there is very little evidence that natural disasters such as earthquakes, floods, and hurricanes have any connection with human sinfulness. To maintain that these events would not take place in a sinless world, or that only those who deserve it are punished in this way, is theologically gratuitous.

2. Process Theology:
A Loving God in a Developing Universe

The classical Augustinian theory of evil presupposed a God who is all-powerful and all good. Many modern thinkers find themselves unable to accept this assumption as a basis for justifying the existence of suffering in the world. As we have seen, it was John Stuart Mill who put the dilemma most bluntly: if God is able to prevent evil and does not, then God is not good. If God would prevent evil and cannot, then God is not almighty.

In general, there are two ways in which some contemporary thinkers have attempted to respond to Mill's articulation of the dilemma and thereby to change the traditional perspective on the problem of evil. One is to alter the usual understanding of the divine and to maintain that although the creator is all-good and all-wise, God is not all powerful. The other way is to alter the traditional understanding of the world, and to assert that *this* world in which we actually exist is intrinsically impossible without some form of failure and suffering.

Many process theologians tend to adopt the first of these stances, namely, that the creator of the universe is an all-loving, creative presence which is intimately involved in the unfolding of history, but that the evolutionary journey is itself beyond his control. In oversimplified terms, process thinkers claim that God loves us and continues to reach out to us in salvific ways. But the universe, once it was initiated in its developmental process, is, in a profound sense, beyond the control of God. If one must choose, these thinkers seem to be saying, between a God who is all-powerful but unmoved by human suffering or a God who is all-loving but not able to take suffering away, it makes more sense to choose the latter.

The intellectual vision of the Anglo-American mathematician and philosopher Alfred North Whitehead has been one of the primary shapers of process theology. Its contemporary proponents have included several Protestant theologians such as Charles Hartshorne, John B. Cobb, Jr., David Griffin, and the Canadian-American theologian and Anglican priest, W. Norman Pittinger. What these thinkers have in common is an openness to the findings of modern science, tempered by the spirit of divine involvement, human freedom, and the theme of journey, all of which are characteristic of the Hebrew/Christian scriptures. Justice and compassion are no less important themes for process thinkers than are growth and energy. The reason for this is that process thought is far less abstract than classical metaphysics; hence it tends to value the relational experience between concrete individuals as the basis for interpreting the wider universe.

On a popular level the process perspective has been compassionately articulated by Rabbi Harold Kushner in his widely read book, *When Bad Things Happen To Good People*. As a young theology student, Kushner spent a great deal of time trying to understand the Book of Job. Later, as a small town rabbi, he counseled other people through pain and grief. But it was only when he learned that his three-year-old son Aaron would die in his early teens of a rare disease that he confronted the mystery of suffering in his own life. His reflections are both personal and pastoral, and though he does not explicitly locate his perspective in the process tradition, it becomes clear that he at least shares its basic assumptions about God's role in human life and pain.

Process thinkers respect the evolutionary nature of reality and attempt to come to terms with suffering and evil within that framework. They also replace the distant cosmic God of the Deists with a compassionate and creative presence at the heart of the evolutionary process. Their perspective and their reasoning are in many ways insightful and compelling. In the end, however, their vision is difficult to square with the biblical emphasis on a transcendent God who is clearly in charge of creation's origins and destiny and who freely chooses to enter into a loving and redemptive relationship with the creatures of the universe.

3. *Irenaeus Revisited:*
Redemptive Pain in a Developing World

In the medieval theology of evil and suffering, the writings of St. Irenaeus were either entirely neglected or were considered to be an eccentric point of view which had been espoused by a few of the early church fathers. In our time, however, the Irenaean perspective, which for centuries had been an overlooked "minority report," has gained widespread recognition and actually forms the core vision for a fresh interpretation of the problem of evil. One of the primary reasons for the rediscovery of Irenaeus is the shift which has taken place in contemporary theology from the metaphysical framework of the Middle Ages to a teleological perspective which places more significance on the categories of history, development, process, and the evolution of human experience.

We have already outlined the basic vision of Irenaeus in Chapter Three. In this section we will explore the ways in which his thought has been reclaimed and developed in new directions by contemporary theologians. The process theologians, as we have seen, alter the traditional approach to the problem of evil by proposing a God who, although lovingly and creatively involved in the journey of history, is not able to shape its ultimate destiny or prevent suffering among its creatures. The Irenaean tradition, on the other hand, respects the biblical understanding of God as all-good and all-powerful; but it defines the world itself in a radically developmental way. If we assume a creation which is in process and human beings who are gifted with free will and responsibility, then some forms of failure, tragedy, and suffering are inevitable.

In this world-view suffering is not an absurd intruder into the universe nor even the result of a fall from some preternatural state of happiness. Suffering is the byproduct of growth, the price of creation's journey toward completion. John Hick, one of the major proponents of the Irenaean perspective today, speaks of the ways in which human beings must grow toward wholeness through their struggle with the evolving energies of the universe and with the moral evil which flows from human sin and its consequences. This means that the sinfulness from which humans are redeemed by divine love and the suffering which flows from that sinfulness have their own paradoxical place within God's providence. This is not the same as saying that God is the source of evil and suffering or that he introduced them into creation out of some divine sense of sadism. Evil and suffering are realities to be overcome and fought against. Their place, as Hick points out, "is not something that ought to exist but something that ought to be abolished." The mystery of God's love for us is that the redemptive process turns "all things unto good," even human brokenness and the selfishness of our lives.

One of the major Catholic exponents of the Irenaean approach is Matthew Fox, O.P., whose "creation-centered spirituality" is an influential if controversial alternative to the "fall-redemption" theology which has, until recently, tended to dominate Western Christianity. Fox and the other scholars associated with the Institute for the Study of Creation-Centered Spirituality have refocused the creative and expansive role which suffering can have in the journey toward spiritual maturity. In his book *Original Blessing,* Matthew Fox describes suffering as a dimension which is "built into the birth process of the entire cosmos." Suffering is an integral dimension of the sacrifice and yielding, the receiving and birthing forth, which is essential for human self-realization and the encounter with the divine.

4. Teilhard de Chardin: Creative Suffering

Perhaps no 20th century thinker has better articulated the Irenaean approach to suffering and evil than Pierre Teilhard de Chardin. His impact on contemporary theology and church teaching is so significant that I have chosen to summarize his thought separately. In actuality Teilhard's vision goes beyond the Irenaean perspective and can rightfully be considered a Christian anthropology for our age.

When Teilhard died in New York City in 1955, the French Jesuit priest and paleontologist was little known outside a circle of fellow priests, scientists, and friends. Today he is a symbol of the winds of change which have swept through the Catholic Church in the last several decades. By attempting in essays, books, and lectures to reconcile science and religion, Teilhard became part of a wider theological controversy which is still unfolding in the post-Vatican II church. During his lifetime Teilhard was prohibited from publishing his vision and its implications. In 1957 the Holy Office banned his works from Catholic bookstores and subsequently issued a *monitum* regarding some aspects of his thought.

Ironically, there is now strong evidence that his theological perspective was one of the dominating influences behind what many consider to be Vatican II's most important document: *Gaudium et Spes,* "The Pastoral Constitution on the Role of the Church in the Modern World." One commentator goes so far as to say that Teilhard is "the hidden footnote" for this entire council document.

What is so startling and insightful about Teilhard's thought? Why has it been controversial while at the same time influential in shaping contemporary church teaching? More importantly for our purposes, what is Teilhard's view regarding the meaning of suffering and evil?

In his first published book, *The Phenomenon of Man,* which was completed in 1940, Teilhard depicts evolution as the fundamental unfolding of the universe—a journey divinely conceived and therefore irresistible—from elemental matter through the advent of life, animal consciousness, and human thought toward God. "Human beings did not descend from apes," Teilhard was fond of saying; "they ascended."

In Teilhard's system evolution is not just a philosophical or theological hypothesis; it is the key to the meaning of existence. It operates not through blind chance, as most of the scientific materialists argued, but purposefully through the creative intent of a loving God. The starting point of evolution from primordial matter Teilhard called Alpha, and its goal or destiny he referred to as the Omega Point. Omega is, in effect, God; but Alpha also carries the divine presence within it. Thus, the universe began in God and will return to God, with human consciousness and freedom playing a vital role in the evolutionary journey. Human beings, Teilhard insisted, "are not the static center of the world, but the axis and arrow of evolution." The future of the creative journey is somehow mysteriously dependent upon the manner in which human persons exercise their freedom and responsibility both individually and communally.

Until recently scientists have tended to interpret the growth of the universe as a sequence of combinations in what Teilhard describes as the "Outside of Things:" atoms forming molecules, molecules forming cells, cells forming plants and animals. According to scientific theory, however, these changes manufacture no new energy. The classic law of thermodynamics claims that the new organism expends its energy in heat and eventually disintegrates.

Most physicists reckon that the sun, for example, will consume all of its available hydrogen atoms in about 15 billion years, then cool off and die. In effect this means that the story of the universe is a quiet cosmic requiem.

Teilhard rejected this prospect of a dying universe as contrary to the creative intention of God. He was convinced that there is another form of energy which is capable of producing higher forms of life and which counteracts the tendency toward universal decay. The French paleontologist and mystic looked for such an energy on the "Inside of Things," by which he meant consciousness; and he ascribed some form of inherent consciousness even to the lowest forms of inorganic matter. This "Inside of Things" or consciousness is what Teilhard calls "radial" or spiritual energy, separate from but related to "tangential" energy (the Outside of Things). Thus Teilhard reversed the law of thermodynamics and replaced it with the "law of complexity-consciousness."

According to this theory, complexity increases on the "outside" until prevented by the loss of tangential energy. But on the "inside," radial energy, which is inexhaustible, drives the organism toward higher levels of both complexity and consciousness. In the evolution of animals this process reached a "critical threshold" in human beings as instinct and awareness broke through to the level of thought, moral judgment, freedom of choice, and spirituality. Human beings thus become the "arrow" or leading edge of evolution, since in them evolution has, for the first time in history, become conscious of itself.

Through the interplay of tangential and radial energy, Teilhard reinterpreted evolution and the history of the universe. Geologists have traditionally spoken of the successive layers of the earth in terms of the barysphere (composed of metals), the lithosphere (rocks), the hydrosphere (water), and the biosphere (various life-forms). From Teilhard's vantage point there is another layer of the earth: the noosphere (from the Greek *nous,* mind), which represents the "thinking layer" of the earth's development. But the noosphere is not the apex of evolution. Beyond it, Teilhard believed, there is a call to a further series of syntheses converging toward the Omega Point. The prerequisite to this final ascent is human freedom and its response to God's redemptive love in what Teilhard refers to as "Christogenesis." Radial energy finds its highest expression in the power of Christian love—an energy which can ultimately move the universe toward its destiny in God.

Where does the reality of evil find a place in this hope-filled (some would say overly optimistic) view of creation? What role does the experience of personal and communal suffering have in the evolution of consciousness and love? Is there any reason to hope that human beings will accept responsibility for the future of the earth's growth?

These were questions which haunted Teilhard throughout his life. If he was hopeful about the universe as a whole, Teilhard was far from an optimist in his daily life. He bore with patience his personal trials and the rejection of his writings by the church, but his friends often found him depressed and even on the verge of despair. The pages of *The Divine Milieu* are filled with poignant lines on the "passivities of diminishment" and the need to unite our sufferings with those of Christ. There was nothing naive or abstract about Teilhard's approach to pain and evil. "Suffering is to be treated as an adversary and fought against right to the end,'' he wrote in 1950; ''and at the same time we must accept it insofar as it can uproot our egoism and center us more completely on God.'' This is the starting point and context for his approach to the mystery of suffering and evil.

In the unfolding of the universe there are three forms of evil which confront us: (1) the suffering which is a by-product of growth; (2) the evil of disorder, failure, and sin; and (3) the ultimate evil of death.

The Pain of Growth. There cannot be progress in the direction of higher consciousness without struggle and effort. This is especially true in the case of human persons for whom the struggle becomes self-directing and conscious. By our very nature we must decide about the meaning of our lives. We set goals for ourselves and instinctively yearn to expand our awareness and our gifts. This also means that we are keenly conscious of the price we pay to realize those goals and to pursue our values. Teilhard points out that the drive toward self-transcendence also carries with it the temptation to drop out or to give up. The movement of life is upward; and precisely because we can reflect upon this direction of movement, we are capable of experiencing both the difficulty of the ascent and the natural inclination to halt. There is a joy in growth that distracts us from the pain, but the pain is always there. The suffering which is a consequence of growth is inevitable in an evolutionary world.

The Evil of Disorder and Failure. Most of us, if we have basic psychological and emotional health, can accept the cost of growing. We develop the realism and even the wisdom of knowing that nothing of value in life comes easily. But it is a different story when we must face obstacles which are beyond our control or confront our inability to attain the goals which we have set for ourselves. At some point in most of our lives we encounter the absurd and apparently futile aspects of life.

In Teilhard's understanding of the world this encounter with the evil of disorder and failure is also inevitable. A universe in evolution and a world without some disorder is contradictory. The problem resides not in the creator but in the structure of created being. If someone were to give us a bouquet of flowers, we would probably be surprised to find several sickly blossoms, since they were picked one by one and assembled with artistic design. On an ordinary tree in the forest, however, we would be surprised not to find some broken branches and deformed limbs. We would simply accept these as signs of the tree's struggle to grow through the hazards of climate and time. Similarly, in a universe which is still in process we can expect that there will be encounters with disorder and personal experiences of failure. The world, Teilhard writes, is "an immense groping;" and the price of its search is suffering as it is encountered in people's lives.

The Evil of Death. But what of the ultimate evil of death? How can there be any meaning in the process of extinction which seems to occur all around us? Not all the branches of a tree are broken or deformed, but in the end all of them must die. In the same way, every human person must face death, whether he or she is rich or poor, just or unjust.

As we have seen, Teilhard postulates the need for a

divine personal Omega, whose existence guarantees the ultimate success of evolution. In an evolutionary process in which we are destined to reach perfection in God, death must in some mysterious way contribute to the growth of our personality. The experience of death is a metamorphosis between two different stages of our personality. It is a "critical point" in our personal evolution, in which our radial energy (our deepest interior self) experiences the limitations of tangential energy and confronts a new threshold of being. By passing through the "death barrier" we are transformed into a new relationship with God and the rest of reality. According to Teilhard death is not so much a separation of matter and spirit as it is the occasion of a new relationship between them.

Whether or not this understanding of death has philosophical and theological validity, it obviously cannot account for the deeper mystery that each of us faces in the experience of dying. In his approach to reality, Teilhard attempts to integrate the findings of science with the vision of faith. Human reason led him to postulate a transcendent personal Center for the evolutionary process. His Christian faith led him to identify this Center with Jesus of Nazareth. In the end it is the pattern of Christ's suffering and dying which gives meaning to the suffering and death of Christians.

5. Liberation Theology: A Prophetic Stance Toward Evil

For Teilhard de Chardin the former metaphysical perspective on theology had given way to a more horizontal or historical view. This point of view, which he shared with several other European theologians, has had a pronounced influence on the Second Vatican Council and subsequent church teaching. The problem of evil was now understood in terms of the *telos,* or goal, of human history. This expanded the mystery of suffering and evil beyond the individual to embrace dimensions of community, social progress (or regress), and the responsibility of human beings to further the evolutionary process.

In moving from metaphysics to process, theology has likewise shifted away from the intellectualism of Thomism to a "neo-voluntarism" which stresses will, action, and love as responses to evil in the world. It is in light of this emphasis on historical responsibility and the renewed commitment to action that we can understand the emergence of various political theologies in Europe and the theology of liberation in Latin America. From one point of view the theology of liberation is an extension of Teilhard's approach to theology; from another point of view it is a reaction against it.

Gustavo Gutierrez, perhaps the most articulate of the liberation theologians, has criticized Teilhard de Chardin's theology as being too politically neutral and detached from the suffering of the poor and the oppressed. His criticism extends beyond Teilhard to the other European thinkers who have developed a more historical and process-oriented approach to theology. According to Gutierrez these theologies tend to be too preoccupied with Christian anthropology in terms of science and religion, but insufficiently concerned with relationships in human society as they involve the social, economic, and political realities of people's lives.

The content of Teilhard's writings and some of the church's recent documents would, in some ways, be similar to liberation theology in that they address the issues of socialization, human progress, freedom, and the dangers of totalitarianism. But they do so in what Gutierrez describes as the "style of doctrinal or systematic theology" rather than out of a stance of prophetic commitment. The emphasis in liberation theology is on the prophetic rather than the systematic or the teleological understanding of evil.

This is true not only of Latin American liberation theology but to some extent of other theologies of liberation (African theology of liberation, U.S. black theology, and theological reflections on the role of women). Liberation theology begins with the life and circumstances of people; it reflects on concrete problems as a basis for gaining pastoral insight and active commitment. It is more concerned about "orthopraxy" (truth-to-be-done) than it is about "orthodoxy" (doctrinal or systematic truth).

The Latin American theology of liberation became a coherent and recognized movement within the Catholic Church when the Latin American bishops (CELAM) met in Medellin, Colombia, in the fall of 1968. At this meeting, the leaders of the Latin American church sought to read the signs of the times in the light of their faith and to respond with a pastoral plan of action. What emerged from Medellin was nothing less than a new understanding of sin and a prophetic approach to overcoming evil.

What is this new understanding of sin? What impact has liberation theology had on the church's approach to suffering and evil?

To answer these questions we must examine both the method and the vision of liberation theology. At Medellin the assembled bishops did not deal with developing countries in general, as did Paul VI's encyclical *Populorum Progressio* or Vatican II's *Gaudium et Spes*. They explored the unique history and circumstances of the people and church of Latin America. This reflects the method of liberation theology. It begins with the concrete reality, the lived experience of human beings. It then moves from the practical situation in which people find themselves to a pastoral reflection on this situation in the light of biblical faith. Finally, from the insights gained through this theological reflection it returns to the practical circumstances with pastoral options and strategies for action.

Thus the starting point of the Medellin conference was not the institutional church, but oppressed persons—the pilgrim church in exile. The church at Medellin understood itself less as an authoritarian teacher and more as a servant called into solidarity with the poor. It is no longer just a church for the poor or even with the poor, but a church which finds its identity and vision *from* the poor. Through this solidarity of discernment the believing community confronts injustice; and, through positive social programs, it seeks to change sinful and violent institutional structures.

What does liberation theology mean by sinful structures or systemic violence? In the centuries following the Reformation, Catholic moral theology tended to focus on the obligations of the individual to avoid evil and to do good. The moral theology manuals which were used in most seminaries usually evaluated human acts in isolation from their circumstances and without much regard for their wider relational meaning. These same manuals relied heavily on scholastic principles as a basis for judging the moral worth or sinfulness of individual acts and used scripture only as "proof texts" to illustrate their ethical axioms.

In contrast, liberation theology begins with the lived situation of individuals and emphasizes their relationship to the wider circle of people and social structures in which they find themselves. The Word of God is not used as an incidental tool to buttress rational arguments, but as the prophetic vision within which the social and pastoral reflection is carried out. The fundamental biblical thematic for liberation theology is the *exodus*—the journey which transformed a ragged band of slaves into the people of God.

Yahweh freed Israel from oppression; and even though the Hebrew people chose other forms of slavery by turning aside from the covenant of freedom, God continued to offer them the hope of a final liberation. The prophets constantly summoned them to recognize and resist the forms of injustice which so often oppressed them, and helped them to envision a final exodus which was still to come. The liberation theologians see this ultimate "passing over" to freedom as realized in the life, death, and resurrection of Jesus of Nazareth and in the paschal mystery as it lives in the Christian community. In this they echo the conviction of Pope John Paul II that "salvation means liberation from evil."

The exodus theme connotes a different understanding of sin and freedom than is found in the moral manuals of the last few centuries. Christian freedom is liberation from sin, but sin is found as much in the structures of human society as it is in the hearts of individual persons. It is not enough to focus on our personal moral growth, since our sinful choices have consequences that go far beyond ourselves. We may even find ourselves in situations which are systemically violent even though we are not aware of any direct subjective guilt on our part. The theology of liberation focuses on this wider, institutional evil which is often hidden beneath socially and culturally legitimized forms of oppression. We find examples of such sinful structures in segregation, apartheid, sexism, racism, and all other forms of institutionalized discrimination. We encounter the most radical forms of oppression in situations where there is an unjust distribution of wealth and in social structures which reinforce the powerlessness of the poor, the homeless, and the starving.

In the past few years there have been two significant developments in regard to the theology of liberation. On the one hand, the institutional church has become increasingly concerned about some activists, who, in their desire to implement pastoral guidelines for liberation, have become involved in what appear to be purely political activities with little or no religious dimension. In some Latin American countries this has led to painful divisions in the church community—divisions which only intensify the political and social tension which is already present.

Ironically, during the very time in which some of the practitioners and theologians of liberation have come under suspicion by the official church, the vision of liberation theology has continued to influence ecclesial teaching on social justice and the problem of evil. In the fall of

1971, the Synod of Bishops, in their document *Justice in the World,* integrated many of the concerns of liberation theology and even adopted much of its language. The document assumes the reality of structural sin and describes injustice as a social reality which must be denounced and resisted. Action on behalf of justice is characterized as an integral and essential dimension of the Christian gospel, rather than an afterthought or footnote in the life of the church.

In similar fashion, the influence of liberation theology can be seen in Paul VI's *Octogesima Adveniens* ("A Call to Action," 1971, issued on the 80th anniversary of Leo XIII's *Rerum Novarum*) and in his landmark encyclical on evangelization, *Evangelium Nuntiandi* (1975). Both documents reiterate the Christian mandate to liberate women and men from their unjust social and political conditions as well as their personal brokenness. In 1974 the Synod of Bishops issued a statement emphasizing the church's mission to promote "the integral salvation of man, his full liberation." Even the recent cautionary statements of the Vatican regarding liberation theology presuppose the basic principles of Medellin and the Latin American theologians. Even as it warns about certain excesses the Vatican fundamentally affirms the vision of liberation theology.

6. The Lord of the Absurd: The Protest Against Evil

The question of evil and suffering arises, as we have seen, on two basic levels. On the philosophical or theoretical level it is encountered as a *problem* which confronts our minds and imaginations and cries out for some reasonable answer. On the personal or existential level evil is confronted as a *mystery,* as a lived experience of pain or deprivation, for which there can never be an adequate explanation. Both the mind's desire to know why and the heart's need to enter the mystery must be honored. As pilgrims on life's path we alternate between our demand for rational answers and the realization that all theory falls short. In the face of suffering, our finest intellectual efforts are, to use the image of Thomas Aquinas, like so much straw waiting to be burned.

Today, as in biblical times, there are those who claim that the only authentic stance before evil and suffering is that of radical protest. The more hopeful among them would allow for a desperate, blind faith in a God whose mystery and reality are beyond the parameters of human reason. But many of them can best be characterized as "protesting agnostics." Writers such as Elie Wiesel and Richard Rubenstein, who are both victims and survivors of the Holocaust, place little value in theodicies or theological arguments, however well nuanced, which attempt to give meaning to human suffering.

In their rejection of the classical explanations of the problem of evil, these thinkers continue the ancient biblical tradition of protest which is found in the writings of Job and Ecclesiastes. In his book *After Auschwitz,* Rubenstein speaks of the impossibility of theological reflection in the traditional sense; and instead he puts God on trial for the utter senselessness of human anguish in this century. Another Jewish writer, John K. Roth, develops the image of God as "repenting" in the face of the atrocities and darkness of this century.

Many of these thinkers find their philosophical roots in the existentialist movement, but instead of dismissing life as meaningless, they engage in an intense struggle with God and the reality of pain. They may put aside the value of philosophical theory, but they do not stop wrestling with the scandal of human violence and the apparent absence of God. If anything, they engage in a kind "hand to hand combat" with the mystery of suffering and evil.

The Roman Catholic thinker who most ably articulates this protest tradition is Raymond J. Nogar, O.P., a popular teacher and lecturer in the United States until his death in 1968. In his book *The Lord of the Absurd,* Nogar rejects the theological attempts to make sense of evil in the Catholic tradition, and emphasizes the importance of the leap of faith as the only adequate response to the mystery of suffering. From the standpoint of secular history, the story of salvation is rationally preposterous. There is no reasonable explanation for a God who chooses a handful of disorganized Jewish tribes, in a backward part of the world, and then molds them into his chosen people. It is even more incredible that this same God would become incarnate, suffer, die, and rise from the dead, thereby transforming the entire meaning of existence.

If the story of salvation is irrational to the atheist or the agnostic, is it any more intellectually appealing to the believer? Nogar's answer is clearly in the negative. Despite the fact that Teilhard de Chardin and other modern theologians have attempted to make Christianity more acceptable to the modern scientific mind, the paradox of human pain and the enigma of Christianity still remain. God does not enter human life as the expected one, but as "an Intruder, the Uninvited Guest upsetting every expectation."

The scientist might be able to count on the regular motions of the heavens, and the philosopher can speculate upon the order in the universe; but there is not the slightest expectation, according to Nogar, that we can rest our meaning or the direction of our lives on this cosmic harmony. It is only the leap of faith which makes Christian life possible. And it is the power of faith which enables us to carry the cross of suffering in the face of rational absurdity.

7. Evil and Suffering in an Apocalyptic Perspective

Eschatology refers to that part of theology which studies the tension between the "now" and the "not yet." It explores the final goal (the Greek word is *eschaton*) of history, which in some mysterious way is hidden in the pain and possibilities of the present. Biblically speaking, eschatology is a theological reflection on the theme of promise and fulfillment—our trust in divine providence and our reliance upon the covenant which will transform our darkness into light. Finally, in terms of the problem of evil, eschatology describes the chasm between things-as-they-are and things-as-they-ought-to-be. Given this framework, each of the theological stances which we have outlined regarding the mystery of suffering and evil is eschatological. The important question, of course, is related to the particular manner in which they account for the polar tension between the "now" and the "not yet." In other words, how or in what manner are they eschatological?

In biblical literature there are two basic stances toward the final promise of God, or the *eschaton*. One of these traditions finds its expression in the prophetic movement, especially during the classical era from Elijah to Jeremiah. The second stance is the apocalyptic tradition, which began to appear as early as the writings of Ezechiel, Joel, and the second part of Zechariah, but which came to full expression in Daniel, the Book of Revelation, and other intertestamental writings.

What is the difference between the prophetic and the apocalyptic traditions? How does this difference affect the manner in which they respond to the problem of evil? The classical prophets, such as Isaiah and Jeremiah, felt a powerful call from God to read the signs of the times and to call the people of their age to conversion. Their enduring message is "Return to the Lord!" This mandate for change is also what makes the prophetic tradition distinctive in biblical history. In their call to conversion the prophets were not only addressing individual people and their personal ethics; they were challenging the entire community of Israel to change their way of thinking and living, and thereby to change the shape of history. It is this conviction regarding the religious responsibility for history which is characteristic of the prophetic understanding of eschatology.

The prophets were involved in the social concerns of their age, many of which had obvious political dimensions. They believed that an authentic change of heart among the leaders and people would transform the direction of the future. Thus the prophetic response to the tension between the "now" and the "not yet" was to respond to God's call by confronting evil in oneself and in one's societal structures and to cooperate in the work of bringing about the messianic kingdom. We can recognize in the prophetic tradition some of the key elements which became the motivating vision of contemporary liberation theology and its response to the mystery of evil.

The apocalyptic tradition takes a different stance toward history and the problem of evil. Its assumptions about history arise from a context of crisis, and its response to crisis is to abandon human responsibility in favor of divine judgment. We can trace the origins of apocalyptic literature to the post-exilic experience of Israel, somewhere around 200 B.C.E. This was a time of great political, social, economic, and religious upheaval. Those who survived the ordeal of the exile and came straggling back to begin rebuilding their homeland, had to face the broken dreams of the past. The sweeping promise of a Davidic line of rulers, which the people had carried in their national consciousness for centuries, together with the political and cultural prestige which it implied, was dead. In the face of all this brokenness, where could the people turn for hope? Where could they find meaning and the motivation to confront evil?

The apocalyptic writers appealed to a people in the midst of crisis and on the edge of despair. The energy which they were able to mobilize and the vision which they developed is strikingly different from the prophetic tradition. The prophets called on their contemporaries to turn away from selfishness and private needs in order to become involved in the concerns of their age. The apocalyptic writers, in contrast, proclaimed that human history had collapsed into the domain of darkness. The presence of evil had become so dominative that neither political nor religious activity on behalf of justice would make any difference. Only the direct intervention of God's vengeance could bring about the messianic era.

Having abandoned any direct human role in shaping the future, the apocalyptic writers look beyond history and the framework of human experience for salvation. Their writings abound with images of the heavenly sphere where angels and other intermediaries bring encouragement to human pilgrims in the midst of their pain and suffering. They describe a cosmic struggle which is being waged beyond the limited confines of human history, a battle in which God alone can bring salvation from the demonic powers which hold the earth and its people in bondage.

It is from these transcendent visions and images that this tradition receives its name: *apocalypsis*—the "uncovering" or revealing of that which is held secret from the evil realm of the world and reserved for God's chosen ones as a source of consolation and hope. The key element of this secret is that those who are suffering from the powers of evil can expect an imminent end to human history and to the world. This *eschaton* will occur through a great cosmic catastrophe which will be the occasion of widespread violence, fear, and human suffering. Following this period of great crisis, however, there will come a new age, a dramatic act of salvation through the direct intervention of God, which will usher in the final state of glory for those who have remained faithful.

Both the apocalyptic and the prophetic approaches to evil and salvation were integrated into the canon of scriptures and subsequently into the teaching of the church. In the life of Christians throughout the ages, these two perspectives have maintained a creative tension between the human responsibility to struggle against evil, on the one hand, and the conviction, on the other hand, that the final direction of history is in the hands of God. If the prophet interprets the signs of the present as a call to help shape the future, the apocalyptic Christian speaks instead about the future that is breaking into the present—God's future for the world and its salvation.

Recent church teaching, as we have seen, tends to emphasize the prophetic role of Christians to struggle against moral evil through a vision which works for peace and programs that struggle for justice. Many of the major theologians of our time have pursued the prophetic perspective in preference to the apocalyptic as a context for their writings. Even those who have taken the apocalyptic stance seriously (such as Wolfhart Pannenberg) have not explored its implications for the traditional problem of evil. All the same, the apocalyptic stance continues to be a valid aspect of the church's tradition. Even as Vatican II called Catholic Christians to a more active and responsible role in resisting evil and building the reign of peace, it did not set aside the church's apocalyptic perspective. Today, as in the past, it acknowledges that God is the Lord of history; beyond the human forms of sinfulness, there are demonic forces at work in the world (cf., for example, *Gaudium et Spes,* #13; Constitution on the Sacred Liturgy, #6).

In some segments of the church community today it is the apocalyptic perspective which carries the most theological weight and offers greater consolation and hope. Given the historical circumstances of our times, this is not surprising. We live in an era of crisis and upheaval not unlike that in which the apocalyptic form of literature was born. As we approach the beginning of the third millenium of Christian history, the spiritual and emotional encounter with cosmic anxiety will, if anything, be intensified and heightened. The apocalyptic response to suffering and evil will very likely continue to have a significant place in Catholic life, especially on the level of popular devotions and personal piety. If Christian apocalyptic has been neglected by contemporary theologians, it finds a strong following in some areas of Catholic piety (e.g. devotion to Our Lady of Fatima) and is an integral part of the theology of the Catholic charismatic renewal.

8. *New Approaches to the Meaning of Death*

Traditionally, Catholic theology has defined death as "the separation of body and soul." This description focuses on the passive or receptive aspect of dying; it emphasizes that death is something which happens *to* us. When the physiological conditions which are necessary for the continuation of life are no longer present, there is little that anyone can do about it. Even the most sophisticated life-support systems and the latest medical technology eventually become unable to sustain or simulate the circumstances which enable life. At that moment we are pronounced medically dead. In religious language we say that the soul leaves the body. This is the passive dimension of death, a violent, almost shocking aspect of its mystery. From the purely external point of view, a living being undergoes death as an end, a term, a point beyond which that organism no longer continues to exist.

While respecting this passive dimension of death as an inevitable occurrence in the human life-cycle, several recent theologians, such as Karl Rahner, Ladislaus Boros, and Roger Troisfontaines, and medical specialists such as Dr. Elisabeth Kubler-Ross, have focused on the experience of dying as an active experience of the person. They attempt to explore what meaning we bring to the moment of our death by our own personal history, our freedom, and the unique stance which we alone can claim at the moment of our life's passing.

In one sense these thinkers have simply responded to a renewed fascination with the mystery of death in our time. This interest in death and dying comes from several different sources. Some of it is probably due to the bloody and widespread loss of life which has occurred because of two world wars and to enduring anxiety regarding human existence because of widespread international violence. Some of it may arise from the emergence of personalist and existentialist philosophies, which have had a profound impact on religious thinking. Finally, the interest in death as a personal event may well flow from a heightened awareness of the value and interiority of the human person, which is evident in the social and psychological movements of our century.

What insights can we gain from focusing on the active or personal aspect of dying? What implications do these have for a contemporary spirituality of suffering?

A preliminary answer to these questions comes not from exploring the experience of dying but from reflecting on the everyday flow of human life. Because of the nature of our awareness, human persons are daily confronted with mortality and the fragility of life. ''Why do people die?'' Zorba asks his young friend in Kazantzakis' famous novel. And his friend, like most of the rest of us, can only acknowledge his inability to answer this question. This inability to comprehend our mortality is an experience in which we all share. We confront in our daily routine what we cannot solve with our minds or explain with our words:

that we are limited, fragile creatures who cannot stop the flow of time or the inevitability of our dying. All our human possibilities must be seen in the context of death; it is, as the existentialist philosopher Martin Heidegger has written, "the horizon which closes off the future."

At the same time that death places definitive limits on our lives, it also brings into existence a responsibility and an urgency that would not otherwise be there. The precariousness of our lives gives rise to a degree of unity, coherence, and purpose in our living. We do not have unlimited time at our disposal. We have a certain amount of time in which to shape and give meaning to our relationships and our freedom.

Sickness is already a reminder of this precariousness in life; it is a diminishment of those biological forces which sustain us now and which will disappear entirely in death. It is like a forerunner of the process which will lead to our transformation into eternal life. Sickness becomes part of the gradual formation of the self, what Karl Rahner calls the "autogeneration of the person," which is fully achieved only at the moment of death.

In his analysis of the classic definition of death Rahner concludes that it is important but inadequate. Its importance lies in its underlining the soul's continued existence as well as its new relation to the body. But there are also several things that are inadequate about this description of death. The most important of these is its failure to speak of death as a personal and decisively human event. Even as a description of a biological phenomenon it is defective, for it says nothing of death's impact on the relationship between the soul and the world. Rahner's contribution to the contemporary discussion has mainly been his affirmation of death as a radically personal event. Death, he maintains, cannot merely be an external force or reality which invades one's life; it must also be an act in which a person engages. It is in fact the most significant of all one's acts—a moment of consummation, a maturing self-realization which, in some mysterious fashion, embodies the essential meaning of one's life before God.

Questions for Reflection/Discussion

1. What are the strengths and weaknesses of the contemporary Augustinian approach to suffering and evil? Evaluate this perspective from your own experience.

2. How would you evaluate the response of "process theology" to the problem of evil? If possible, give some examples of people whom you know or have read who follow this line of reasoning.

3. Several contemporary theologians (Teilhard, John Hick, Matthew Fox, etc.) have adapted and developed the earlier vision of Irenaeus regarding the role of suffering and evil in creation. Compare and evaluate these various perspectives. Which of them is closest to your own stance of faith?

4. In what way are the prophetic (liberation theology) and the apocalyptic perspectives contrasting approaches to evil? In what way are they complementary? With which of these stances do you most readily identify? Why?

5. Sharing the faith: In a small group setting invite various participants to choose one of the seven or eight approaches to suffering and evil. Summarize and defend your posi-

tion, not just with theological argument, but from your life experience.

Further Reading

Faricy, Robert, "The Problem of Evil in Perspective," *Communion* (Vol. 6:173-191, Summer 1979). This entire issue is concerned with suffering and evil. I am particularly indebted to Fr. Faricy's ideas and insights.

Fox, Matthew, O.P., *Original Blessing: A Primer in Creation Spirituality* (Santa Fe, NM: Bear and Co., 1983).

Gutierrez, Gustavo, *A Theology of Liberation* (Maryknoll, NY: Orbis Books, 1973).

Journet, Charles, *The Meaning of Evil* (New York: Kenedy, 1963).

Kushner, Harold, *When Bad Things Happen To Good People* (New York: Schocken Books, 1981).

Mellert, Robert B., *What Is Process Theology?* (New York: Paulist Press, 1975).

Rahner, Karl, *On The Theology Of Death* (New York: Herder and Herder, 1961).

Rubenstein, Richard L., *After Auschwitz* (Indianapolis: Bobbs-Merrill, 1966).

Teilhard de Chardin, Pierre, *The Divine Milieu* (New York: Harper and Row, 1960). *The Phenomenon of Man,* 1959.

Wiesel, Elie, *The Trial of God,* trans. by Marion Wiesel (New York: Random House, 1979).

Chapter 7

CONCLUSION
The Mystery of the Cross in Our Time

IN his book *Conjectures of a Guilty Bystander,* Thomas Merton describes his transition from the "romantic monk" of the 1950's to the prophetic Christian of the 1960's. It was a painful and creative period in his personal journey: a time when new questions challenged old answers, when new human concerns forced him to re-evaluate the meaning of his Christian vocation; a time when the magnitude and intensity of suffering in the world demanded a different personal response.

Thomas Merton's account of his personal transformation is, in many ways, a profile of Catholic experience in recent decades. Both individually and as a community of faith we have experienced a major transition in our self-understanding and in the way we view the world around us. It has been both a confusing and creative journey, a transformation which is far from completed and certainly not yet fully understood. As in the case of Merton, it is not that our tradition has failed us. Rather, new historical circumstances have challenged us to re-examine our tradition of belief and practice. We have found it necessary to rediscover the primal roots of our tradition in scripture and the life of the early Christian community in order to gain historical perspective on the burning issues of our day. This is not an act of surrender or of betrayal, but a task of re-birth and renewal. The pain and uncertainty

which have accompanied this journey are not a death rat-
tle, but the birth pangs of a new age.

In the preceding pages we have attempted to summarize
this transition in the church's life and experience in one important area of theology: the enduring questions which
surround the mystery of suffering and evil. We have
returned to the Hebrew and Christian scriptures and traced
the development of the problem of evil as it emerges in the
biblical story of salvation. We have re-examined the manner in which the church assimilated the scriptures over the
centuries and attempted to formulate a theological and
doctrinal stance regarding evil. Finally, we have explored
the historical transition in which we presently find ourselves, the recent developments in the church's teaching,
and the on-going theological debate surrounding this issue.

What conclusions can we draw from this reflective
journey? How has the church's teaching been affected by
the needs and challenges of contemporary history? On a
personal level, what can we learn from this study which
will better enable us to enter the mystery of suffering and
to share in the redemptive work of overcoming evil? These
are the issues which we will address in this concluding section.

1. A New State of the Question

Questions about the meaning of suffering and evil are as
old as humankind. Today we carry those perennial questions in our hearts just as did those who have lived before
us. We are anxious about our children's future; we reach
out in compassion to our friends who are sick; we wonder

in the night why so many good people experience so much futile pain. While drinking our morning coffee, we read of earthquakes, plane crashes, terrorist killings, the spread of AIDS, crime in our cities, and suicide among our youth. These tragic events leave bruised bodies and broken hearts in their wake, just as suffering has left a trail of tears and bitterness for nameless centuries. We are reminded again that the pain which surrounds us and the questions which haunt us are as old as the collective human heart.

And yet, without being able to put it clearly into words, we instinctively know that there is something different about our experience. There is something painfully new about the manner in which we wrestle with the problem of evil today. Perhaps it is the element of urgency which has thrust the issues beyond the usual theological and philosophical arenas of debate. Perhaps it has something to do with the anxiety which moves beneath the surface of our lives, for despite the apparent apathy regarding the larger human issues, there is a silent concern which all of us carry in our hearts. Neither the distractions of a consumerist society nor the phenomenon of "psychic numbing" can erase the fundamental caring of the human soul. Perhaps it is related to the more immediate and public nature of tragedy and grief. Telecommunications have had a profound emotional effect on the manner in which we face the realities of war, famine, political injustice, and the prospect of nuclear holocaust. Finally, perhaps our changing attitude toward suffering and evil has something to do with the tension between our technological power and our human fragility.

This tension between scientific promise and human limitations found a tragic symbol on the morning of January 28, 1986. The day had dawned bright and full of promise at the Kennedy Space Center where the crew of seven astronauts on the space shuttle Challenger were poised for what most assumed would be a routine launch. Within seconds after lift-off, however, a tragedy took place which stunned the world and shattered our comfortable assumptions about the advance of technology.

Few of us will forget the scene that was replayed again and again on our television sets: the rocket's powerful thrust at lift-off, the billowing trail of vapors, the radio exchange between mission control and the crew. And then, in the flash of an eye, an explosion and the bright orange ball of flame. Few of us will forget the cheers that turned, in an instant, into cries of anguish and helplessness. "In that tragic moment," wrote one commentator, "the world stood still and human voices fell silent. The computers stopped functioning and the stock market fell."

There have been far worse tragedies than this in the history of humanity. There have been natural disasters and wars which have claimed many more victims and caused far more devastating and widespread suffering. Nor was the crew of the Challenger the first to risk their lives for something greater than themselves. History has lost count of those who have offered up their bodies and souls for what they considered to be a worthy cause.

All the same, there is something painfully distinctive about the Challenger tragedy. There are two aspects of this dramatic incident which make it a symbol of our contemporary encounter with the mystery of suffering and evil. The first is related to the intense, communal quality of grief which resulted from the immediacy of television and the emotional impact of seeing the accident happen before our very eyes. As was the case in the assassination of John F. Kennedy and Martin Luther King, Jr., this event drew millions of people around the world into a common experience of shock and sadness.

The second aspect is perhaps less obvious, but even more important as a symbol of our contemporary response to the problem of evil. On the space shuttle Challenger there was no escape mechanism for the astronauts. Their fate was identified with the fate of their craft. In a strikingly similar way, the fate of the human race is identified with the earth. There is no escape mechanism from history or from the human condition. There is no way for us to turn back the evolutionary process which has brought us to this point. We cannot evade the responsibility we have for the earth, for one another, and for the future. We can no longer elude the paradox or the pain, the promise or the agony of being human and free.

No one wanted the Challenger to blow up. In this case it was human error and mechanical malfunction which brought about the tragedy. Similarly, we can assume that no one wants a nuclear war. And yet the same technology which lifted us into outer space is now developing "star wars" weaponry which will escalate the possibility of global destruction.

To put it simply, the reality and consequences of evil have become more and more dependent on how human beings exercise their power and responsibility. It is no longer so much a question of the evil that can happen to us by fate or the normal course of nature, but of the evil we are capable of inflicting on ourselves and on our world. This startling historical fact is what has changed "the state of the question" regarding the problem of evil. This is, as we have seen previously, the new stage of history into which the human race has entered (*Gaudium et Spes* #5), and the "new moment" which the U.S. bishops describe in their pastoral letter on peace. It is also the new context which frames the contemporary debate regarding evil and human suffering.

2. A New Response of Faith

When the church recognized the new age into which human history was passing, it responded to these "signs of the times" at first with caution, and then with a boldness that has brought about controversy and tension among its members. The classical description of the problem of evil, as it had been enunciated by Augustine and other medieval theologians, was both a theological explanation and a spiritual way of living. Its assumptions were grounded in the scriptural story of salvation and the lives of the early martyrs, who validated the vision of redemptive suffering with their own blood. It was celebrated in the sacramental life of the church as Christians united their personal sufferings with those of the risen Christ.

But this classic understanding of suffering and evil also presupposed a certain view of the world. In addition to the Jewish and Christian sources of scripture, Augustine turned to the concepts of Greek philosophy to give intellectual substance to his arguments. This integration of Christian and Hellenic sources eventually developed into the "medieval synthesis" which has, until recently, been the normative model for expressing Catholic teaching.

The world-view in which the medieval synthesis arose was "metaphysical" in the classical sense of the word; that is, it sought for the enduring and eternal substance of reality beyond the passing phenomena which we see with our eyes and touch with our hands. It likewise presupposed a static view of reality in which matter is understood to be a lesser form of being than spirit, and the world is approached as a "vale of tears," a temporary time of testing, which we endure until we leave it for the eternal home of heaven.

It is this metaphysical and other-worldly setting of medieval theology which is the framework for the traditional understanding of suffering and evil. The world was created good by God, but it is now "wounded" and scarred by the fall of the bad angels and the sin of human beings. Evil is present in the world through the work of the devil and the personal sinfulness of women and men. Suffering is a consequence of this sinfulness, the price we must pay for the darkened state of the world. Through God's loving mercy, however, this brokenness has been redeemed. In the passion and resurrection of Jesus, evil has been conquered and hope has been restored; and when we unite our personal sufferings with those of Christ, they also become redemptive.

This view of suffering and evil is faithful to the biblical data and the early Christian tradition. There is no doubt that it brought comfort and hope to vast numbers of believers throughout the centuries. But it is no longer an adequate response for today's church. We live in a world in which the categories of Greek thought are no longer as helpful as they were for the first millennium and a half of Christianity. The static and other-worldly perspective of medieval theology has given way to an incarnational sense of responsibility for the future. The emergence of historical consciousness in the last two centuries has transformed the horizon of human reflection. In the words of Vatican II, "the human race has passed from a rather static concept of reality to a more dynamic, evolutionary one" (*Gaudium et Spes* #5).

As we have seen earlier, this change in perspective has also led to a change in the manner and focus of church teaching regarding evil and suffering. We can see this different response toward evil beginning to emerge in the early social teachings of Leo XIII and Pius XI, as they summon Christians not just to endure injustices for the sake of a heavenly reward, but to work against inequities for the sake of building the kingdom of God. This call to action in the face of evil reaches its high point in the encyclicals of John XXIII and Paul VI, the documents of Vatican II, the statements of the Synods of Bishops, and most recently in the writings of Pope John Paul II.

The Jesuit theologian Robert Faricy suggests that there is a pattern of development or a "trajectory" in the contemporary church's response to the problem of evil. As it has moved beyond the traditional metaphysical categories the church has turned to three modalities of reflection, each of them with biblical roots, through which it is responding to the mystery of suffering and evil.

a) The Teleological Response. This perspective takes into account the growing awareness of our human accountability for the future. The problem of evil is seen as a call to responsibility for the direction or goal (hence the Greek word *telos*) of history. It is the task of Christians to overcome the blindness and destructive attitudes of the present in order to shape the future according to the vision of the gospel. The teleological stance underlines the creative and redemptive aspects of suffering as the way in which each of us contributes to a world which is still "coming into birth" (Rm 8:22).

The teleological response to evil is articulated by theologians such as Teilhard de Chardin and other process thinkers who have re-articulated the earlier vision of St. Irenaeus. It is embodied in church documents such as Vatican II's *Gaudium et Spes* (The Pastoral Constitution on the Church in the Modern World) and Paul VI's *Populorm Progressio* and *Octogesima Adveniens.*

b) The Prophetic Response. The concerns which the teleological perspective raised in a universal way for the world and humanity soon came to be seen in more specific and concrete situations. As the developing nations struggled to have a more equitable share in global resources, it became clear to many theologians that a new pastoral tool of analysis and action was necessary. This tool emerged particularly in Latin America in the form of liberation theology, a movement which has had a clear impact on the church's attitude and response to evil in the world.

Drawing strongly on the biblical tradition of the prophets and their call to conversion, liberation theology has influenced the wider church's commitment to become more active in making peace and building justice. The prophetic response emphasizes the call to hear the cries of the suffering and to make a conscious "option for the poor." It is only through solidarity with the victims that the church can imitate Jesus in becoming a redemptive servant of humanity. The prophetic response is articulated in the Medellin Documents (1968) of the Second General Conference of CELAM (Latin American Episcopate), Pope Paul VI's encyclical *Evangelium Nuntiandi* (1975) on evangelization, the document *Justice in the World* from the 1971 Synod of Bishops, and some of the speeches of Pope John Paul II at Puebla, Mexico. It is also found in the "Instruction of Certain Aspects of Liberation Theology," which the Vatican issued in 1984.

c) The Apocalyptic Response. During a time of upheaval and historical transition such as we are presently experiencing, the limits of our human efforts are even more obvious than our achievements. In some ways the burden of freedom and responsibility only intensifies this experience of dread and helplessness. Thus, the apocalyptic response toward evil is one of radical dependency on God. This biblical and theological stance focuses on God's ultimate power over history. God is not indifferent to suffering, to violence, to pain, or to evil in the world. Beyond the shifting fortunes of human history the world has a sacred purpose, but only God knows this destiny and God alone will bring history to its final goal.

This radical dependence on God in no way lessens the seriousness of human freedom and dignity. The believing community cries out to God against oppression and the persecution of the innocent; its prayer and concern rise up against sin and human misery. For those who look to the apocalyptic vision, the last judgment is an image which expresses how seriously God takes human responsibility. Human beings do indeed have the power to choose—so much so, that in the end we will pass judgment on ourselves through the pattern and meaning of our decisions.

The apocalyptic response has a long and respected presence in Catholic theology and devotional life. Its roots are deep in scripture and in the perennial teaching of the church. It is the same tradition which in our time is approaching the problem of suffering in terms of the universal lordship of the risen Jesus, the power of the Holy Spirit over the powers of darkness, and the Christian victory over evil spirits. Though it has not been one of the principal elements of recent church teaching on evil, the apocalyptic stance remains a vital dimension of popular piety, and, in the instance of the Catholic charismatic renewal, an integral part of Christian life.

3. Continuity Within Change

In the past 25 years there has been a tidal wave of change and development in the life of the church. When Pope John XXIII called for an "aggiornamento" (an updating) in the church's life, it is likely that even he did not realize the scope and consequences of such an endeavor. As we draw near to the beginning of the third millennium of Christian history, there are signs that the institutional church wants to moderate and even curb the rapidity with which the ecclesial structures are changing.

Perhaps the best indicator of the current attitude of the church toward evil and suffering is the speeches and

writings of Pope John Paul II. While accepting the fundamental premise of both the teleological and prophetic
responses, he clearly intends to moderate their philosophical and political focus by emphasizing the transcendent
aspects of faith and religious experience. There is even an
effort on John Paul's part to re-interpret the classical
theology of suffering and evil in terms of today's needs.
We have already analyzed his apostolic letter *Salvifici
Doloris* (On the Christian Meaning of Human Suffering)
in a previous chapter. Since it is one of the most recent official Vatican statements on the question of suffering, we
may well see it as symbolic of the current attitude of the
church toward the problem of evil.

Theologically speaking, *Salvifici Doloris* can best be
described as "centrist," in that it addresses the reality of
suffering on both the level of personal piety and in the
broader scope of global needs. It draws deeply from the
traditional scriptural and theological approaches to suffering, while at the same time building on the historical and
societal awareness of Vatican II and subsequent church
documents. In short, Pope John Paul II has endeavored to
integrate doctrinal continuity with the recent developments
in the church's teaching regarding suffering and evil.

4. The Mystery of the Cross

Despite the progress which technology has brought to
our world, it has not been able to remove the spectre of
disease and starvation. Whatever new insights theology has
developed into the meaning of Christian life, it cannot take
away the pain of those who suffer. "The poor you will

have with you always," Jesus told us; and he might have added many other groups of people as well. They are all still with us: the mothers who watch their children starve, the innocent victims of war, the political prisoners who are tortured, the spouses who mourn the loss of their partners, the victims of disease and earthquakes, the street people and the drug addicts, the broken-hearted and the empty-handed. We know all too well that the experience of suffering will continue to be part of the human journey.

Obviously this does not mean that progress in both technology and theological reflection is insignificant. It only reminds us that in the end we can only embrace the mystery which envelops us. It is reasonable to assume that science will pursue the means to improve the physical well-being of the human species. We can also assume that theology will continue to reflect on the gospel response to evil and its consolation for those who are in pain. But in the midst of it all there will be people who suffer without any apparent purpose and with little consolation. In the face of this reality both science and theology fall silent. "I feel closer to what language cannot reach," Rilke once wrote. Perhaps that is why most of us find ourselves strangely silent in the presence of pain. Is there any other experience which is so close to our depths and yet so far beyond the reach of our words?

The Letter to the Hebrews reminds us that "at various times in the past and in various different ways, God spoke to our ancestors through the prophets; but in our own time, the last days, he has spoken to us through his Son" (He 1:1). It appears that God has always wanted to tell us something about divine compassion—some word of consolation for our brokenness, or an answer to the riddle of suffering and evil. It also appears that God tried just about every available means of finding the "right word"—from the splendor of creation to the poetry of the prophets— without the desired effect. In these last days, God has spoken through his Son. Jesus, as we have learned, is the Word made flesh; he is the "right word" and the "last word" which God has addressed to us.

If there is ever to be an answer to suffering, it must be in this Word, Jesus. And yet, even here we are left wondering what the answer is, or if there is any answer at all. Nowhere in his preaching does Jesus promise to take away pain or suffering. At no time in his healing ministry does he indicate that he will eradicate pain. In fact, he assures us that if we are willing to follow him, we will also "drink from the cup of sorrow" (Mk 10:35-40). The only answer Jesus gives to suffering and evil is to take it on his shoulders and carry it into death. Only then is there resurrection and the transformation of death into new life.

Jesus is God's way of telling us how evil can be overcome and how suffering can be redemptive. If we find this "solution" to the problem of evil to be intellectually unsatisfying, it need not surprise us. If we cannot grasp its theological significance, we ought not to be disappointed. The cross is, in the end, not an answer at all, but a *way;* and we are "followers of the Way." We can never know the redemptive meaning of suffering unless we are willing to make the same journey.